Christian Lorentzen is an editor at the *London Review of Books*.

The *n+1* Anthology

–

SAY WHAT YOU MEAN

Notting Hill Editions

Published in 2012 by Notting Hill Editions Ltd
Newcombe House, 45 Notting Hill Gate
London W11 3LQ

Designed by FLOK Design, Berlin, Germany
Typeset by CB editions, London

Printed and bound
by Memminger MedienCentrum, Memmingen, Germany

A CIP record for this book is available from the British Library

ISBN 978-1-907-90356-4

www.nottinghilleditions.com

Contents

Christian Lorentzen

– Introduction –

I n 2004 we were all so young. 'Fallujah' was a word you often heard, so were the words 'swift boat'. Photographs showed that American soldiers had a way with hoods and leashes. Facebook was a small business on a college campus. Susan Sontag was dying, and Saddam Hussein was on trial. I was working at a little magazine that had been started by socialists in the 1920s, had no website, and was, though I didn't know it, a few months away from closing. I'd never sent or received a text message, and I still had most of my hair.

In the basement of an industrial building under the Manhattan Bridge in Brooklyn, another magazine was being born. Despite its name, *n+1* was to be a literary magazine, not a journal of mathematics. Four of the editors had thrown in $2,000 a piece that would go mostly towards production. A party was thrown to raise another $2,000 in $20 subscriptions. I showed up during production of the first issue to proofread, write headlines, and show the editors how to make a table of contents. I brought my sister Allison along; just out of college and with a natural talent for soothing egos while cracking whips, she was enlisted as the managing editor. All of us had been through big schools and some of us had moved commas around at venerable magazines, but we were marginal. (Marginality would prove to be an advantage.) It's not the way of the world to let young people say anything about anything important. And there was the fact that no one involved was being paid. And when you're writing otherwise than for money, there's no point but to say what you mean, and to write as well as you can. So, eight years later and an ocean away, it's worth quoting at length from the editors' opening statement, from the first page of *n+1*'s first issue:

We are living in an era of demented self-censorship. The old private matters – the functions of the body, the chase after love and money, the unhappiness of the family – are now the commonest stuff of public life. We are rotten with confession. But try saying that the act we call 'war' would more properly be termed a massacre, and that the state we call 'occupation' would more properly be termed a war . . . or that the political freedoms so cherished and, really, so necessary, are also the mask of a more pervasive, insidious repression – try saying all this, or any of it, and see how far you get. Then try saying it in a complex way, at some length, expressing as you do so an actual human personality.

The last sentence would become the magazine's imperative. And the contents of this anthology show that for the editors and the writers who've come into the magazine's orbit, the original principles still hold.

Who were the editors? They were grad students

with a surplus of energy and so far uncompromised by worldly success. Keith Gessen, a Moscow-born high-school football star, had for years been mixing journal-ism with odd jobs, and was a familiar face to Boston art-house movie-goers (he'd sold them tickets at the box office). Mark Greif, the house philosopher, came to the table with a fistful of homeless polemics. Ben-jamin Kunkel, a child of the Rockies who'd done time as a rancher, had a book deal already, for his comic socialist bildungsroman. Chad Harbach had a novel in gestation, about college baseball players in his native Wisconsin, that would seven years later become a best-seller. The four of them had gone to Harvard together during the 1990s. (I was there too, younger than them and, as happens at that age, in awe of them.) Marco Roth, the only native New Yorker, had studied with Derrida and was getting a PhD at Yale alongside Greif. The first issue was very much the work of friends and family (Gessen's sister Masha, already an accomplished journalist, was a contributor), which is how you have to operate under conditions of obscurity and austerity. The first masthead had eleven names; current versions have more than thirty.

The first issue established a format that has held up for fifteen numbers: up front a series of unsigned salvos on "the Intellectual Situation"; lengthier essays and fiction under various rubrics in the middle; a few reviews in the back. The opening section, referred to as "the IS" in house, became a distinguishing, perhaps notorious, feature from the start. In the first issue, which bore the word 'Negation' on the spine, the IS featured attacks on other magazines, including the 'designated haters' of the *New Republic*; the child-fetishizing 're-gressive avant-garde' of *McSweeney's* (which had just moved from Brooklyn to San Francisco, vacating ter-ritory *n+1* would annex). The question was: how to be neither permanently 11 years old, nor already your own grandfather?

The first thing was to avoid nostalgia. The maga-zine has never run articles about dead people, but has instead brought a sense of history to focus on present circumstances. It would also avoid imitation, no aping the Vorticists' *Blast* or Mencken's *American Mercury*. (One upshot of this method was the drab design of the first issue: a black logo on a maroon background, with a few headlines in a blobby white box. Design-ers and people who knew about art had to be found.) Which isn't to say the magazine wasn't aware of im-portant predecessors. *The Baffler*, which through the 1990s had chronicled the way corporate America had subsumed the counterculture, was then on hiatus after its office in Chicago had burned down and its founder, Thomas Frank, had become a best-seller and one of the most prominent voices of the American left. In terms of fiction, another magazine started in the 1990s, *Open City* had fostered many young writers who'd applied scrutiny to the conditions of their lives in and around New York, and Sam Lipsyte, an *Open City* mainstay, contributed an excerpt of his novel *Home Land* to the first issue of *n+1*.

Another magazine that was on everybody's mind was *Partisan Review*. On the one hand its legacy was immense: Delmore Schwartz, Dwight Macdonald, Mary McCarthy, Edmund Wilson. (A fight at a party between a couple of *n+1* writers in Keith Gessen and Chad Harbach's kitchen circa 2005: 'You think you're Edmund Wilson and I'm Mary McCarthy, but it's the other way around.') On the other hand, the magazine hadn't been very interesting since Susan Sontag's heyday in the 1960s, and it had ended up neoconservative. You could draw a line, not necessarily straight, from *Partisan Review* to Fallujah.

So we were on our own. But pretty soon there were more of us. One thing missing from the start was women writers and editors. Aside from my sister and Keith's sister, there weren't any involved in the first issue. 'Where is Elif Batuman?' Keith asked me one day. She'd written the stuff we most admired in college. She was at Stanford, getting a PhD, but she wanted to do another kind of writing. The 18,000 words of 'Babel in California' arrived in time for the second issue, and turned out to be the core of what would become *The Possessed*, her memoir of youth under the spell of Russian literature. And many other brilliant women followed. The magazine now has its own radical feminist research collective.

We also had to find readers. Besides the internet,

the most effective method seemed to be to throw a party, in a high school gym or a disused can factory, often with a loud band. The beer was cheap, and came in bottles, many of which I opened myself. The parties sold issues and raised funds, except the one where the cash box was stolen (rumor has it, to start another magazine). There was also the internet. The magazine was always a project avowedly pursued on paper, but that can't be the only way a magazine exists anymore. So a website (nplusonemag.com) was started, very much in an ad hoc way. Somewhere between issues one and two we realized that certain topics (Wes Anderson, anal sex) could draw an enormous (by little-magazine standards) readership, but it also proved a good training ground for new writers and a worthy place for writing that was of the moment, as in a particular moment tomorrow afternoon. Aside from a couple of parodies, *n+1* never started a blog, though the internet generally, especially its effect on writing, has become one of the magazine's perennial subjects. And the website was not the only significant offshoot. An art magazine, *Paper Monument*; a web-based book review, *N1BR*; a broadsheet film review, *N1FR*; and in the last year the broadsheet *Occupy Gazette* have all taken on lives of their own. The Occupy movement quickened the magazine's pulse, and earned many young staffers, through furious activity, places at the top of the masthead; it also bonded the magazine to upstart publications on the left like *Triple Canopy*, *Jacobin*, and the *New Inquiry*. And there have been books, about the financial crisis, about hipsters, about art, and about poverty and debt.

The magazine has taken some knocks, not least from the mighty James Wood himself, whose response to the editors' opening attack appeared in the third issue: 'it was itself a wholly negative attack on negativity. There I was, waiting for the sweets of positivity, for the proposals and manifestos and counterarguments, only to find the merest dusting of kiddies' sugar . . . Positive individuality; the cultivation of "something new" (anything, as long as it is something?); a connection to the Great Tradition; and . . . youth! One of the editors, Keith Gessen, could be found on the last page of the magazine writing: "It is time to say what you mean." Indeed, but what do you mean? The Editors had unwittingly proved the gravamen of their own critique: that it is easier to criticize than to propose.'

As I hope this anthology shows, he spoke too soon. Besides proofreading, bartending, and grunt work unloading boxes of issues and moving the office from one cheap space to another across town, most of my experience with *n+1* has been as a writer. Meanwhile, I've made my living editing and writing for publications that pay. Those sorts of publications tend to pressure writer and subject into one or another corner: say that x is the best thing ever, or say it's the worst thing ever; say that it's something totally new, or declare its death. The editors of *n+1* tend to encourage their writers to linger on a subject, to pursue it personally and at great length through many, many drafts, into a story that can't be boiled down, despite the magazine's algebraic name, into an equation. The magazine's beginning was a setting up of a few imperatives and restraints. Since then it's been a matter of writing through the gaps.

This book collects writings by the founding editors, from Mark Greif's 'Against Exercise' in issue one to Benjamin Kunkel's 'Political Psychopathology' in issue 15. Greif's essay is the first of his many ventures in writing on private matters (here, body functions) without resorting to rotten confession. (Greif is the only editor who hasn't yet published a book, but two volumes are expected soon.) Writings on politics and actual politicians are naturally ephemeral: Kunkel's essay diagnoses the America of Obama and Romney. The way that writers live and literature seeps into life is one of *n+1*'s permanent topics: here Keith Gessen's essay on writers and money, Marco Roth's study of the 'neuronovel,' Chad Harbach's 'MFA vs. NYC,' and Elif Batuman's reading of the Best American Short Stories series convey a view of the scene from inside; Carla Blumenkranz's study of the website Gawker rounds out the picture with an anatomy of the new para(site)-literature. 'Female Trouble,' Elizabeth Gumport's study of the experimental writer Chris Kraus, is a newer turn, the first major effort of *n+1*'s radical feminist wing. And Nikil Saval's essay on Occupy as a labor movement shows how, when the moment arrived, the magazine was ready to do its thinking on the streets.

Three more pieces – by Emily Witt, Wesley Yang, and Kristen Dombek – are representative of what may be the core of *n+1*'s achievement: they are long, mix the public and the private, sprawl over America, and are formally sui generis efforts by writers who came to the magazine out of the blue. It is easier to criticize than to create something new. That takes years.

Mark Greif

– Against Exercise –

Were 'In The Penal Colony' to be written today, Kafka could only be speaking of an exercise machine. Instead of the sentence to be tattooed on its victims, the machine would inscribe lines of numbers. So many calories, so many miles, so many watts, so many laps.

Modern exercise makes you acknowledge the machine operating inside yourself. Nothing can make you believe we harbor nostalgia for factory work but a modern gym. The lever of the die press no longer commands us at work. But with the gym we import vestiges of the leftover equipment of industry into our leisure. We leave the office, and put the conveyor belt under our feet, and run as if chased by devils. We willingly submit our legs to the mangle, and put our stiffening arms to the press.

It is crucial that the machines are simple. The inclined planes, pins, levers, pulleys, locks, winches, racks, and belts of the Nautilus and aerobic machines put earlier stages of technical progress at our disposal in miniature. The elements are visible and intelligible for our use but not dangerous to us. Displaced, neutralized, they are traces of a necessity which no longer need be met with forethought or ingenuity. A farmer once used a pulley, cable, and bar to lift his roofbeam; you now use the same means to work your lats.

Today, when we assume our brains are computers, the image of a machine-man, whether Descartes's or La Mettrie's, has an old and venerable quality, like a yellowed poster on the infirmary wall. Blood pressure is hydraulics, strength is mechanics, nutrition is combustion, limbs are levers, joints are ball-in-socket. The exercise world does not make any notable conceptual declaration that we are mechanical men and women. We already were that, at least as far as our science is concerned. Rather it expresses a will, on the part of each and every individual, to discover and regulate the machine-like processes in his own body.

And we go to this hard labor with no immediate reward but our freedom to do it. Precisely this kind of freedom may be enough. Exercise machines offer you the superior mastery of subjecting your body to experimentation. We hide our reasons for undertaking this labor, and thoughtlessly substitute a new necessity.

No one asks whether we want to drag our lives across a threshold into the kingdom of exercise.

Exercise is no choice. It comes to us as an emissary from the realm of biological processes. It falls under the jurisdiction of the obligations of life itself, which only the self-destructive neglect. Our controversial future is supposed to depend on engineered genes, brain scans, neuroscience, laser beams. About those things, we have loud, public, sterile debates – while the real historic changes are accomplished on a gym's vinyl mats, to the sound of a flywheel and a ratcheted inclined plane.

In the gym you witness people engaging in a basic biological process of self-regulation. All of its related activities reside in the private realm. A question, then, is why exercise doesn't stay private. It could have belonged at home with other processes it resembles: eating, sleeping, defecating, cleaning, grooming, and masturbating.

Exerciser, what do you see in the mirrored gym wall? You make the faces associated with pain, with tears, with orgasm, with the sort of exertion that would call others to your immediate aid. But you do not hide your face. You groan as if pressing on your bowels. You repeat grim labors, as if mopping the floor. You huff and you shout and strain. You appear in tight yet shape-less lycra costumes. These garments reveal the shape of the genitals and the mashed and bandaged breasts to others' eyes, without acknowledging the lure of sex.

Though we get our word gymnasium from the Greeks, our modern gym is not in their spirit. Athletics in the ancient institution were public and agonistic. They consisted of the training of boys for public contests. The gymnasium was closest to what we know as a boxing gym, with the difference that it was also the place adult men gathered to admire the most beautiful boys and, in the Greek fashion, sexually mentor them. It was the preeminent place to promote the systematic education of the young, and for adults to carry on casual debates among themselves, modeling the intellectual sociability, separated from overt politics, that is the origin of Western philosophy. Socrates spent most of his time in gymnasia. Aristotle began his philosophical school in the covered walkway of a gymnasium.

The Socratic and Peripatetic methods could find little support in a modern gym. What we moderns do there belongs to mute privacy. The Greeks put their genuinely private acts into a location, an oikos, the household. To the household belonged all the acts that sustained bare biological life. That included the labor of keeping up a habitation and a body, growing food and eating it, bearing children and feeding them. Hannah Arendt interpreted this strong Greek distinction of the household from the public sphere as a symbol of a general truth, that it is necessary to keep the acts which sustain naked life away from others' observation. A hidden sphere, free from scrutiny, provides the foundation for a public person – someone sure enough in his privacy to take the drastic risks of public life, to think, to speak against others' wills, to choose, with utter independence. In privacy, alone with one's family, the dominating necessity and speechless appetites could be gratified in the non-thought and ache of staying alive.

Our gym is better named a 'health club,' except

that it is no club for equal meetings of members. It is the atomized space in which one does formerly private things, before others' eyes, with the lonely solitude of a body acting as if it were still in private. One tries out these contortions to undo and remake a private self; and if the watching others aren't entitled to approve, some imagined aggregate 'other' does. Modern gym exercise moves biology into the nonsocial company of strangers. You are supposed to coexist but not look closely, wipe down the metal of handlebars and rubber of mats as if you had not left a trace. As in the elevator, you are expected to face forward.

It is like a punishment for our liberation. The most onerous forms of necessity, the struggle for food, against disease, always by means of hard labor, have been overcome. It might have been naïve to think the new human freedom would push us towards a society of public pursuits, like Periclean Athens, or of simple delight in what exists, as in Eden. But the true payoff of a society that chooses to make private freedoms and private leisures its main substance has been much more unexpected. This payoff is a set of forms of bodily self-regulation which drag the last vestiges of biological life into the light as a social attraction.

The only truly essential pieces of equipment in modern exercise are numbers. Whether at the gym or on the running path, rudimentary calculation is the fundamental technology. As the weights that one lifts are counted, so are distances run, time exercised, heart rates elevated.

A simple negative test of whether an activity is modern exercise is to ask whether it could be done meaningfully without counting or measuring it. (In sports, numbers are used differently; there, scores are a way of recording competition in a social encounter.) Forms of exercise which do away with mechanical equipment, as running does, cannot do away with this.

In exercise one gets a sense of one's body as a collection of numbers representing capabilities. The other location where an individual's numbers attain such talismanic status is the doctor's office. There is a certain seamlessness between all the places where exercise is done and the sites where people are tested for illnesses, undergo repairs, and die. In the doctor's office, the blood lab, and the hospital, you are at the mercy of counting experts. A lab technician in a white coat takes a sample of blood. A nurse tightens a cuff on your arm, links you to an EKG, takes the basic measurements of your height, and weight – never to your satisfaction. She rewards you with the obvious numbers for blood pressure, body-fat ratio, height and weight. The clipboard with your numbers is passed. At last the doctor takes his seat, a mechanic who wears the white robe of an angel and is as arrogant as a boss. In specialist language, exacerbating your dread and expectation, you may learn your numbers for cholesterol (two types), your white cells, your iron, immunities, urinalysis, and so forth. He hardly needs to remind you that these numbers correlate with your chances of survival.

How do we acquire the courage to exist as a set of numbers? Turning to the gym or the track you gain the anxious freedom to count yourself. What a relief it can be. Here are numbers you can change. You make the exercises into trials you perform upon matter within reach, the exterior armor of your fat and muscle. You are assured these numbers, too, and not only the black marks in the doctor's files, will correspond to how long you have to live. With willpower and sufficient discipline, that is, the straitening of yourself to a rule, you will be changed.

The gym resembles a voluntary hospital. Its staff members are also its patients. Some machines put you in a traction you can escape, while others undo the imprisonment of a respirator, cueing you to pump your lungs yourself, and tracking your heart rate on a display. Aided even by a love that can develop for your pains, this self-testing becomes second nature.

The curious compilation of numbers that you are becomes an aspect of your freedom, sometimes the most important, even more preoccupying than your thoughts or dreams. You discover what high numbers you can become, and how immortal. For you, high roller, will live forever. You are eternally maintained.

The justification for the total scope of the responsibility to exercise is health. A further extension of the counting faculty of exercise gives a precise economic character to health. It determines the anticipated numbers for the days and hours of one's life.

Today we really can preserve ourselves for a much longer time. The means of preservation are reliable and cheap. The haste to live one's mortal life diminishes. The temptation toward perpetual preservation grows. We preserve the living corpse in an optimal state, not that we may do something with it, but for its own good feelings of eternal fitness, confidence, and safety. We hoard our capital to earn interest, and subsist each day on crusts of bread. But no one will inherit our good health after we've gone. The hours of life maintenance vanish with the person.

The person who does not exercise, in our current conception, is a slow suicide. He fails to take responsibility for his life. He doesn't labor strenuously to forestall his death. Therefore we begin to think he causes it.

It may be a comfort to remember when one of your parents' acquaintances dies that he did not eat well or failed to take up running. The nonexerciser is lumped with other unfortunates whom we socially discount. Their lives are worth a percentage of our own, through their own neglect. Their value is compromised by the failure to assure the fullest term of possible physical existence. The nonexerciser joins all the unfit: the slow, the elderly, the poor, and the hopeless. 'Don't you want to 'live?" we say. No answer of theirs could satisfy us.

Conceive of a society in which it was believed that the senses could be used up. Eyesight worsened the more vivid sights you saw. Hearing worsened the more intense sounds you heard. It would be inevitable that such a conception would bleed into people's whole pattern of life, changing the way they spent their days. Would they use up their powers on the most saturated colors, listening to the most intoxicating sounds? Or might its members refuse to move, eyes shut, ears covered, nursing the remaining reserves of sensation? We, too, believe our daily lives are not being lived, but eaten up by age. And we spend our time desperately. From the desperate materialist gratifications of a hedonistic society, commanding immediate comfort and happiness, we recoil to the desperate economics of health, and chase a longer span of happinesses deferred, and comforts delayed, by disposing of the better portion of our lives in life-preservation.

Exercise does make you, as a statistical person, part of different aggregate categories that die with less frequency at successive ages. It furnishes a gain in odds. This is the main public rationale for those billions of man- and woman-hours in the gym. The truth, however, is also that being healthy makes you feel radically different. For a segment of its most ardent practitioners, exercise in its contemporary form is largely a quest for certain states of feeling. A more familiar phenomenon than the young person who is unhappy physically from never exercising is the young exerciser who suffers from missing one or two days of exercise. The most common phenomenon may be the individual who judges, in his own mind if not out loud, the total healthiness of his state at each moment based on what he ate, what he drank, how much he exercised, when, with what feelings as he was doing it, and with what relation to the new recommendation or warning he just heard on the news hour's health report. One feels healthier even when the body doesn't feel discernably different. Or the body does begin to feel different – lighter, stronger, more efficient, less toxic – in ways that exceed the possible consequences of the exercises performed. This may be a more important psychic 'medicalization of human life' than anything a doctor can do with his tests.

The less respectable but even more powerful justification for day-to-day exercise is thinness. It involves the disciplining of a depraved will, rather than the righteous responsibility to maintain the health of the body-machine and its fund of capital.

Women strip their bodies of layers of fat to reveal a shape without its normal excess of flesh. Despite the new emphasis on female athleticism, the task of the woman exerciser remains one of emaciation. Men thin themselves, too, but more importantly bloat particular muscles, swelling the major clusters in the biceps, chest, and thighs. They awaken an incipient musculature that no work or normal activity could bring out in toto. Theirs is a task of expansion and discovery. Women's emaciation is a source for feminine eye-rolling and rueful nicknames: the 'social X-ray,' the actress as skin and bones. Men's proud expansion and discovery of six muscles of the lower abdomen, reminiscent of an insect's segmented exoskeleton, likewise becomes a byword and a joke: the 'six-pack,' bringing exercise together with the masculinity of drinking.

Unlike the health model, which seems to make a continuous gain on mortality, thinness and muscle-expansion operate in a cruel economy of accelerated loss. Mortality began when the first man and woman left the Garden. Everyone has to die, but no one has to shape a physique, and once body-altering begins, it is more implacable than death. Every exerciser knows that the body's propensity to put on weight is the physical expression of a moral fall. Every exerciser knows that the tendency of the body to become soft when it is comfortable or at rest, instead of staying perpetually hard, is a failure of discipline. This is the taste of our new Tree of Knowledge. In our era of abundance, we find that nutrition makes one fat rather than well-fed, pleasures make one flabby rather than content, and only anorexics have the willpower to stop eating and die.

Exercise means something other than health to a young person who conceives sexual desirability as the truth about herself most worth defending. And youth is becoming permanent, in the demand that adults keep up an outward show of juvenile sexuality. The body becomes the location of sexiness, rather than clothes or wit or charisma. This is less true for society – which values personality still – than for the exerciser herself, who imagines an audience that doesn't exist. Saddest of all is the belief that an improved body will bestow bliss on the unloved.

The shock troops of modern exercise are women just past the college years. Only recently the beneficiary of a sexually mature body, and among our culture's few possessors by native right of the reduced body type we prefer – which we daily prefer more openly, more vehemently – the girl of twenty-two is a paradoxical figure as an exemplar of exercise. She is not yet among the discounted. But she knows her destiny. She starts immediately to get ahead in the race to preserve a form that must never exceed the barest minimum of flesh. A refreshing honesty can exist among exercisers who are not yet caught up in the doctrine of health. The rising incidence of smoking among young women, which worries public health advocates, is coincident with the rising incidence of gym exercise, which doesn't. While the cigarette suppresses appetite (rebelliously), the stairmaster attacks calories (obediently). Each can become intensely, erotically pleasurable, and neither is really meant for health or longevity.

The doctrine of thinness introduces a radical fantasy of exercise down to the bone. It admits the dream of a body unencumbered by any excess of corporeality. Thanatos enters through the door opened by Eros, and exercise flirts with a will to annihilate the unattractive body rather than to preserve its longevity. Without an accompanying ideology of health, thinness would in fact liquidate all restraints, generating a death's-head vision of exercise. Health curiously returns as the only brake on a practice that otherwise would become a kind of naked aggression against the body.

With health in place, the aggression is more likely to be carried on psychically. It pools, then starts an undercurrent of hatred for this corrupt human form that continually undoes the labor you invest in it. One-hundred twenty pounds of one's own flesh starts to seem like the Sisyphean boulder. Yet the bitterness of watching your body undo your work is restrained by a curious compensation which Sisyphus did not know. If the hated body is the scene of a battle, a certain pleasure still emerges from the unending struggle, and, in a hedonistic order divided against its own soft luxuries, at least this pleasure, if no other, can be made to go on forever.

An enigma of exercise is the proselytizing urge that comes with it. Exercisers are always eager for everyone else to share their experience. Why must others exercise, if one person does?

No one who plays baseball or hockey demands everyone else play the sport. Sports are social. Their victories become visible in the temporary public arrangements of a game. Perhaps accomplishments recognized by others in the act of their occurrence can be left alone. The gym-goer, on the other hand, is a solitary evangelist. He is continually knocking on your door, to get you to recognize the power that will not give him peace. You, too, must exercise. Even as he worries for your salvation, nevertheless, he has the gleam of someone who is ahead of you already, one chosen by God.

Running is most insidious because of its way of taking proselytizing out of the gym. It is a direct invasion of public space. It lays the counting, the pacing, the controlled frenzy, the familiar undergarment-outergarments and skeletal look, on top of the ordinary practice of an outdoor walk. One thing that can be said for a gym is that an implied contract links everyone who works out in its mirrored and pungent hangar. All consent to undertake separate exertions and hide any mutual regard, as in a well-ordered masturbatorium. The gym is in this sense more polite than the narrow riverside, street, or nature path, wherever runners take over shared places for themselves. With his speed and narcissistic intensity the runner corrupts the space of walking, thinking, talking, and everyday contact. He jostles the idler out of his reverie. He races between pedestrians in conversation. The runner can oppose sociability and solitude by publicly sweating on them.

No doubt the unsharability of exercise stimulates an unusual kind of loneliness.

When exercise does become truly shared and

mutually visible, as in the aerobics that come close to dance, or the hardcore bodybuilding that is always erotic and fraternal, it nears sport or art and starts to reverse itself. When exercise is done in a private home, or in untenanted landscapes, or without formal method, apparatus, or counting, it recovers certain eccentric freedoms of private techniques of the self.

However, the pure category of modern exercise is concerned not with the creative process of reproduction (as in activities-in-common), nor the pure discoveries of solitude (as in private eccentricity). It pursues an idea of replication. Replication in exercise recreates the shape and capabilities of others in the material of your own body, without new invention, and without exchange with others or crossing-over of material between selves.

It is a puzzling question, in fact, whether 'you' and 'your body' are the same in exercise. If on the one hand exercise seems strongly to identify exercisers with their bodies, by putting them to shared labor, on the other hand it seems to estrange them from the bodies they must care for and manage. Where does 'fitness' actually reside? It seems to be deep inside you; yet that inside has risen to a changeable surface. And this surface is no longer one you can take off, as you did a costume in earlier methods of improving your allure. Fashion historians point out that women freed themselves from corsets worn externally, only to make an internal corset, as they toned the muscles of the abdomen and chest, and dieted and exercised to burn away permanently the well fed body that whalebone stays temporarily restrained. Though the exerciser acts on his self, this self becomes ever more identified with the visible surface. Though he works on his body, replication makes it ever more, so to speak, anybody.

Does this critique imply a hatred of the body? On the contrary. The ethos of gym exercise annihilates the margin of safety that humans have when they relate to their own bodies. Men and women seem more ashamed of their own actual bodies in the present environment of biological exposure than in a pre-gym past. An era of exercise has brought more obsession and self-hatred rather than less.

A feminist worry becomes important. It is certainly possible to make people used to displaying to others' eyes the biological processes of transformation. And this has been, at times, the aim of feminists, who intended to attack a patriarchy that vilified the natural body or that made biological processes a source of shame and inferiority. But the forms of exposure which have recently arisen are not in line with feminist liberation of the unconditioned body.

Patriarchy made biology a negative spectacle, a filth that had to be hidden. The ethos of exercise makes it a positive spectacle, a competitive fascination that must be revealed. The rhetoric of 'loving the body' can thus be misused. With the extension of the cliché that one should 'not be ashamed' of the body, people are less able to defend themselves against the prospect that their actual bodies, and biological processes, may be manifest at every moment, in new states of disciplining neither public nor private. It becomes a retrogression, a moral failing in these people, to wish to defend against exposure, or to withdraw their health, bodies, arousal, and self-regulation from the social scene, as if privacy of this kind were mere prudery or repression.

Once subjected to this socialization of biological processes, the body suffers a new humiliation no longer rooted in the distinctions between the revealed and the hidden, the natural and the shameful, the sexual ideal and the physical actuality, but in the deeper crime of merely existing as the unregulated, the unshaped, the unsexy, the 'unfit.'

Our practices are turning us inside out. Our hidden flesh becomes our public front. The private medical truth of bodily health becomes our psychic self-regard. Action in public before strangers and acquaintances has disappeared from the lived experience of the citizen and been replaced by exercise in public, as speech gives way to biological spectacle.

Your exercise confers superiority in two contests, one of longevity and the other of sex. Facing mortality, the gym-goer believes himself an agent of health – whereas he makes himself a more perfect patient. Facing the sexual struggle, the gym-goer labors to attain a positive advantage, which spurs an ever receding horizon of further competition.

The technical capabilities of gym exercise in fact drive social ideals and demands. The exerciser conforms, in our era's most virulent practice of conformism. But exercise itself pushes medicine and sexual allure toward further extremes. The feedback does not stabilize the system but radicalizes it, year by year. Only in a gym culture does overweight become the 'second leading cause of death' (as the news reported this spring) rather than a correlation, a relative measure, which positively covaries with the heart attacks, the cancers, the organ failures and final illnesses that were formerly our killers. Only in a gym culture do physical traits that were formerly considered repellent become marks of sexual superiority. (We are hot now for the annihilation by exercise and dieting of once voluptuous feminine flesh, watching it be starved away in natural form and selectively replaced with breast implants, collagen injections, buttock lifts. We've learned to be aroused by the ripped, vein-popping muscles that make Incredible Hulks of men who actually push papers.) Because health and sex are the places we demand our truth today, newly minted ideals must be promulgated as discoveries of medical science or revelations of permanent, 'evolutionary' human desires.

The consequences are not only the flooding of consciousness with a numbered and regulated body, or the distraction from living that comes with endless life-maintenance, but the liquidation of the last untouched spheres of privacy, such that biological life itself becomes a spectacle.

'You are condemned. You are condemned. You are condemned.' This is the chant the machines make with their grinding rhythm, inside the roar of the gym floor. Once upon a time, the authority of health, and the display of our bodies and biological processes, seemed benign, even liberating. We were going to overcome illness, we were going to exorcise the prudish Victorians. But our arrows were turned from their targets, and some of them punctured our privacy.

The thinness we strive for becomes spiritual. This is not the future we wanted. That prickling beneath the exerciser's skin, as he steps off the treadmill, is only his new self, his reduced existence, scratching the truth of who he is now, from the inside out.

Elif Batuman

– Short Story and Novel –

'New American fiction' is, to my mind, immediately and unhappily equivalent to new American short fiction. And yet I think the American short story is a dead form, unnaturally perpetuated, as Lukács once wrote of the chivalric romance, 'by purely formal means, after the transcendental conditions for its existence have already been condemned by the historico-philosophical dialectic.' Having exhausted the conditions for its existence, the short story continues to be propagated in America by a purely formal apparatus: by the big magazines, which, if they print fiction at all, sandwich one short story per issue between features and reviews; and by workshop-based creative writing programs and their attendant literary journals. Today's short stories all seem to bear an invisible check mark, the ghastly imprimatur of the fiction factory; the very sentences are animated by some kind of vegetable consciousness: 'I worked for Kristin,' they seem to say, or 'Jeff thought I was fucking hilarious.' Meanwhile, the ghosts of deleted paragraphs rattle their chains from the margins.

In the name of science, I recently read from cover to cover the Best American Short Stories anthologies of 2004 and 2005. Many of these stories seemed to have been pared down to a nearly unreadable core of brisk verbs and vivid nouns. An indiscriminate premium has been placed on the particular, the tactile, the 'crisp,' and the 'tart' – as if literary worth should be calibrated by resemblance to an apple (or, in the lingo of hyperspecificity, a McIntosh). Writers appear to be trying to identify as many concrete entities as possible, in the fewest possible words. The result is celebrated as 'lean,' 'tight,' 'well-honed' prose.

One of the by-products of hyperspecificity is a preponderance of proper names. For maximum specificity and minimum word count, names can't be beat. Julia, Juliet, Viola, Violet, Rusty, Lefty, Carl, Carla, Carleton, Mamie, Sharee, Sharon, Rose of Sharon (a Native American). In acknowledgment of the times, the 2004 and 2005 volumes each contain exactly one Middle East story, each featuring a character called Hassan. I found these names annoying, universally so. I was no less annoyed by John Briggs or John Hillman than by Sybil Mildred Clemm Legrand Pascal, who invites the reader to call her Miss Sibby. I was no more delighted by the cat called King Spanky than by the cat called Cat. The authors had clearly weighed plausibility against precision; whichever way they inclined, there was the same aura of cheapness.

Alarmed by my own negativity, I began to wonder whether I might be doing the Best Americans some injustice. For a point of comparison, I reread a few stories by Chekhov, who is still the ostensible role model for

American 'short-fiction practitioners.' (Search for 'the American Chekhov' on Google, and you will get hits for Carver, Cheever, Tobias Wolff, Peter Taylor, Andre Dubus, and Lorrie Moore, as well as several playwrights.) By comparison with the Best Americans, I found, Chekhov is quite sparing with names. In 'Lady with Lapdog,' Gurov's wife gets a few lines of dialogue, but no name. Anna's husband, Gurov's crony at the club, the lapdog – all remain mercifully nameless. Granted, Chekhov was writing from a different point in the historico-philosophical dialectic: a character could be called 'Gurov's wife,' 'the bureaucrat,' or 'the lackey,' and nobody would take it as a political statement. The Best Americans are more democratic. Every last clerk, child, and goat has a name.

Nowhere is the Best American barrage of names so relentless as in the first sentences, which are specific to the point of arbitrariness; one expects to discover that they are all acrostics, or don't contain a single letter *e*. They all begin in medias res. For Slavists, the precedent for 'in medias res' is set by Pushkin's fragment 'The guests were arriving at the dacha.' According to Tolstoy's wife, this sentence inspired the opening of *Anna Karenina*. Would Pushkin have managed to inspire anybody at all had he written: 'The night before Countess Maria Ivanovna left for Baden Baden, a drunken coachman crashed the Mirskys' troika into the Pronskys' dacha'? He would not.

Pushkin knew that it is neither necessary nor desirable for the first sentence of a literary work to answer the 'five w's and one h.' Many of the Best Americans assume this perverse burden. The result is not just in medias res, but in-your-face in medias res, a maze of names, subordinate clauses, and minor collisions: 'The morning after her granddaughter's frantic phone call, Lorraine skipped her usual coffee session at the Limestone Diner and drove out to the accident scene instead'; 'Graves had been sick for three days when, on the long, straight highway between Mazar and Kunduz, a dark blue truck coming toward them shed its rear wheel in a spray of orange-yellow sparks.' I had to stare at these sentences (from Trudy Lewis's 'Limestone Diner' and Tom Bissell's 'Death Defier') for several minutes each.

A first line like 'Lorraine skipped her usual coffee session at the Limestone Diner' is supposed to create the illusion that the reader already knows Lorraine, knows about her usual coffee, and, thus, cares why Lorraine has violated her routine. It's like a confidence man who rushes up and claps you on the shoulder, trying to make you think you already know him.

Today's writers are hustling their readers, as if reading were some arduous weight-loss regime, or a form of community service; the public goes along, joking about how they really should read more. Oprah uses identical rhetoric to advocate reading and fitness; Martha Nussbaum touts literature as an exercise regime for compassion. Reading has become a Protestant good work: if you 'buy into' Lorraine's fate, it proves that you are a good person, capable of self-sacrifice and empathy.

Another popular technique for waylaying the reader is the use of specificity as a shortcut to nostalgia – as if all a writer has to do is mention Little League or someone called Bucky McGee, and our shared American past will do the rest of the work. Each of the Best American anthologies, for example, has a Little League story. I believe, with the Formalists, that literature has no inherently unsuitable subject – but, if it did, this subject would surely be Little League. Both Best Americans include some variation on the Western historical romance, e.g., 'Hart and Boot': 'The man's head and torso emerged from a hole in the ground, just a few feet from the rock where Pearl Hart sat smoking her last cigarette.' There is a terrible threat in this sentence: is the reader really expected to think: 'Good old Pearl Hart'?

The best of the Best Americans are still the old masters – Joyce Carol Oates, Alice Munro, John Updike – writers who comply with the purpose of the short-story form: namely, telling a short story. This sounds trivial, but isn't. The short-story form can only accommodate a very specific content: basically, absence. Missing persons, missed opportunities, very brief encounters, occurring in the margins of 'Life Itself': when the content is minimalist, then it makes sense to follow the short-fiction dictates: condense, delete, omit.

Novels, like short stories, are often about absences;

but they are based on information overload. A short story says, 'I looked for x, and didn't find it,' or, 'I was not looking anymore, and then I found x.' A novel says, 'I looked for x, and found a, b, c, g, q, r, and w.' The novel consists of all the irrelevant garbage, the effort to redeem that garbage, to integrate it into Life Itself, to redraw the boundaries of Life Itself. The novel is a fundamentally ironic form; hence its power of self-re-generation. The short story is a fundamentally unironic form, and for this reason I think it is doomed.

When the available literary forms no longer match the available real-life content, the novel can reabsorb the mismatch and use it as material. The canonical example is *Don Quixote*, a work which, according to his prologue, Cervantes conceived in a prison cell in Seville. Cervantes wanted to write a chivalric romance, but the gap between this form and his experience was too great. Then he broke through the formal 'prison': he made the gap the subject of a book.

Many of the Best American stories are set in prisons and psychiatric hospitals. They are trying to break out, but I don't think they will. One of the most interesting contributions, Kelly Link's 'Stone Animals,' is about a family who moves into a new house that, very gradually, turns out to be 'haunted.' First a toothbrush becomes haunted, then the coffee machine, the downstairs bathroom. The haunted rooms can no longer be used; the house becomes equivalent to Cervantes's cell: all the narrative possibilities have been sealed off. The

family has less and less space in which to live. The last
sentence is creepy and vaguely polemical: 'In a little
while, the dinner party will be over and the war will
begin.' Indeed, let the war begin.

Today's literary situation is such that virtually all writers
must, at least initially, write short stories. Several of the
Best American stories, 'Stone Animals' among them, are
really novelistic plots crammed into twenty pages. The
short story is trying to expand into a catchall genre. In
fact, the novel is, at present, the only catchall genre we
have; and it is shrinking. Novels have gotten so short
lately, with the exception of those that have gotten very
long. Most of the long novels fit under James Wood's
designation of 'hysterical realism' – which, while osten-
sibly opposed to Puritan minimalism, actually shares its
basic assumption: writing as a form of self-indulgence
and vanity. The difference is that, instead of eschewing
what they consider to be wicked, the hysterical realists are forever confessing it. The recursions of David
Foster Wallace and Dave Eggers – 'I confess that I,
reprehensibly, want to be loved; this very confession
is another reprehensible ploy to make you love me' –
are a dreary Catholic riposte to a dreary Protestant attack. It would be equally productive for every writer
to start every book with an apology for cutting down
trees which could have been put to better use building
houses for the homeless; followed by a second apology
for the paper consumed by the first apology.

Here is the crux of the problem, the single great-est obstacle to American literature today: guilt. Guilt leads to the idea that all writing is self-indulgence. Writers, feeling guilty for not doing real work, that mysterious activity – where is it? On Wall Street, at Sloane-Kettering, in Sudan? – turn in shame to the no-tion of writing as 'craft.' (If art is aristocratic, decadent, egotistical, self-indulgent, then craft is useful, humble, ascetic, anorexic – a form of whittling.) 'Craft' solicits from them constipated 'vignettes' – as if to say: 'Well, yes, it's bad, but at least there isn't too much of it.' As if writing well consisted of overcoming human weakness and bad habits. As if writers became writers by omit-ting needless words.

American novelists are ashamed to find their own lives interesting; all the rooms in the house have become haunted, the available subjects have been blocked off. What remains to be written about? (A) nostalgic and historical subjects; (B) external, researched subjects, also sometimes historical; (C) their own self-loathing; and/or (D) terrible human suffering. For years, Lorrie Moore has only written about cancer. In *A Heartbreak-ing Work of Staggering Genius*, Dave Eggers implies that anyone who does not find his story compelling is unsympathetic to cancer victims; he describes in gory detail how he plans to eviscerate such people, how he plans to be eviscerated by them in turn. For writers who aren't into cancer, there is the Holocaust, and of course the items can be recombined: cancer and the

Holocaust, cancer and American nostalgia, the Holocaust and American nostalgia. For the last combination, you can't do better than Michael Chabon's *The Amazing Adventures of Kavalier & Clay*, with its memorable opening sentence:

In later years, holding forth to an interviewer or to an audience of aging fans at a comic book convention, Sam Clay liked to declare, apropos of his and Joe Kavalier's greatest creation, that back when he was a boy, sealed and hog-tied inside the airtight vessel known as Brooklyn New York, he had been haunted by dreams of Harry Houdini.

All the elements are there: the nicknames, the clauses, the five w's, the physical imprisonment, the nostalgia. (As if a fictional character could have a 'greatest creation' by the first sentence – as if he were already entitled to be 'holding forth' to 'fans.') Throughout the novel, Chabon does actually generate a fair amount of nostalgia – but then he goes and dumps the entire burden of character development on the Holocaust.

Joe Kavalier is a master magician, an escape artist, a writer of fabulous comic books, a charismatic and fundamentally mysterious person – until, that is, Chabon explains to us that the reason Kavalier became an escape artist was to escape from Hitler. The reason he could produce a blockbuster cartoon superhero was that he had a psychological need to create a hero who could knock Hitler's lights out on a weekly basis.

W. G. Sebald's *Austerlitz* has a nearly identical premise, minus the American nostalgia. It, too, features an authorial stand-in, à la Sam Clay, who finds in some other person a source of narrative. Austerlitz is, like Kavalier, a human enigma who disappears for years on end, leaving trails of clues; in the end, the 'solution' is nothing other than the Final Solution. Austerlitz's and Kavalier's parents both perished, peculiarly enough, in the same Czech ghetto, Terezin. Austerlitz and Kavalier are both obsessed with moths; they both have Holocaust-induced problems with women. (Austerlitz's one love affair, with a woman called Marie, fizzles out during a trip to Marienbad, where he is oppressed by an inexplicable terror; later we understand that it's because he is actually Jewish, and his parents were killed in the Holocaust, and once they went on vacation to Marienbad.)

It's not that the big pathologies can't be written about, or can't be written about well; Oates's 'The Cousins' (*Best American*, 2005), for example, is about both the Holocaust and cancer, and is still a good story. It consists of the letters between two cousins, aging women: one survived the Holocaust and became a famous writer, the other grew up in America and became a retiree in Florida. They were supposed to meet as children, but never did. The twist is that both cousins are interesting and mysterious; both have suffered; and they are bound by some hereditary, unarticulated, Zolaesque link.

Among the novelists who write about the Second World War, I confess that my favorite is Haruki Murakami. Murakami's *The Wind-Up Bird Chronicle* opens with a small, personal mystery – the disappearance of the narrator's cat – which turns out to be related to how the narrator never really understood his wife, who also disappears. The two disappearances are subsequently linked to the occupation of Manchuria, the torture killing of a Japanese soldier, and various other personal and global events. The narrator is moved by all the big historical themes that pass through the novel, but he suffers more immediately from the loss of his cat – as in Brueghel's picture of the farmer ploughing his field while Icarus drowns. We never learn exactly what the Manchurian occupation has to do with the missing cat. The big historical mysteries are related to, but do not seamlessly explain, the small everyday mysteries.

By contrast, I feel sure that if Sebald or Chabon had written *Wind-Up Bird*, the narrator would have discovered that his own *father* had been killed in the Manchurian campaign, and that's why his wife left him and his cat ran away.

Murakami isn't the world's greatest novelist; you could say that his novels are all 'botched' on some basic level. The turns in the plot are often achieved unsatisfyingly, by dreams, or by a character deciding to sit in the bottom of a well; the narrators receive an inordinate amount of oral sex from bizarrely dressed middle-aged women. But botchedness also gives Murakami's novels a quixotic dynamism. Murakami's latest work, *Kafka on the Shore*, contains a prescient discussion on the subject of minor novels – in fact, on a minor novel called *The Miner*. *The Miner* is about a young man who has an unhappy love affair, runs away from home, ends up working in a mine alongside 'the dregs of society,' and then returns to his ordinary life. 'Nothing in the novel shows he learned anything from these experiences, that his life changed, that he thought deeply now about the meaning of life or started questioning society,' Murakami's narrator explains: it is completely unclear why the author decided to write *The Miner* – which makes it particularly valuable to the narrator, by virtue of its very openness.

Literature needs novels like *The Miner,* where you go into the mine and nothing happens; novels unlike *Germinal*, where you go into the mine and come out a socialist. Perhaps modern American literature has kept the worst parts of Zola. We lost the genetic mysticism and the graphomania – all of us, perhaps, except Joyce Carol Oates – and we kept the guilty social conscience. Dear American writers, break out of the jail! Sell the haunted house, convert it to tourist villas. Puncture 'the airtight vessel known as Brooklyn New York.' Write long novels, pointless novels. Do not be ashamed to grieve about personal things. Dear young writers, write with dignity, not in guilt. How you write is how you will be read.

Keith Gessen

– Money –

How much money does a writer need? In New York, a young writer can get by on $25,000, give or take $5,000, depending on thriftiness. A slightly older younger writer – a 30-year-old – will need another $10,000 to keep up appearances. But that's New York. There are parts of this country where a person can live on twelve or thirteen thousand a year – figures so small they can be written out. Of course it depends.

My wife and I moved to New York after college, at 22. We lived in Queens and paid $714 for a one-bedroom apartment (inherited, complete with artist's installation, from my friend, the poet and founder of Ugly Duckling Presse, Matvei Yankelevich). That year, the two of us combined made $24,000. But we had a car, and on weekends we visited my father on Cape Cod. I wrote stories; she organized an art exhibit. We were young.

We moved to Boston. Our rent rose to $900, but it was 1999, even a doorpost could create 'content,' and I was more than a doorpost. I wrote long book reviews for an online magazine that paid 50 cents a word. Our combined income rose to $34,000. I failed to write stories, though; journalism took all my time.

The magazine collapsed with the NASDAQ. We moved to Syracuse and broke up. I stayed on at the MFA program, from which I received $15,000, then $12,000, then $15,000. I wrote stories again. My rent for a two-bedroom apartment was $435.

But I hated Syracuse. I moved back to New York; another friend, a novelist, sublet me his apartment. My rent was $550! That year, with what was left on my graduate stipend, plus some journalism and a book translation ($1,500), I made $20,000. I put $2,000 of it into *n+1*.

I turned 30. Things had to change. I moved to Brooklyn and signed a one-year contract for $40,000 to review books for *New York* magazine. This seemed like so much money that I immediately sent some to my ex-wife, who was back in Boston, with those high rents.

There are four ways to survive as a writer in the US in 2006: the university; journalism; odd jobs; and independent wealth. I have tried the first three. Each has its costs.

Practically no writer exists now who does not intersect as some point with the university system – this is unquestionably the chief sociological fact of modern American literature. Writers began moving into the university around 1940, at the tail end of the Federal Writers' Project, which paid them to produce tour guides of the United States. The first university-sustained writers mostly taught English and composition; in the 1960s and especially the 1970s, however, universities began to grant graduate degrees in creative writing. Now vast regiments of accredited writers are dispatched in waves to the universities or Tucson and Houston, Iowa City and Irvine. George Saunders, the great short story writer and my adviser at Syracuse, told me he knew only two non-teaching writers in his generation (born around 1960): Donald Antrim was one and I forgot the other.

The literary historian Richard Ohmann has argued that the rise of English departments in the 1890s, and their immediate bifurcation into Literature on the one hand and Composition on the other, emerged from a new economy's demand for educated managers. Our own age – born around 1960, and variously called post-industrial, informational, service/consumer – demanded copywriters and 'knowledge workers' and, with the breakdown of traditional social arrangements, behavior manualists (*He's Just Not Texting You*). With the rise of Communications came the rise of Creative Writing, and the new split of English departments into Literature, Creative Writing, and (still) Composition. It's pretty clear by now where this is tending, and which hundred-year-old discipline will become less and less relevant from here on out. We do not have a reading crisis in this country, but we do have a reading comprehension crisis, and with the collapse of literary studies it will get much worse.

For now, the university buys the writer off with patronage, even as it destroys the fundamental preconditions for his being. A full-time tenure-track position will start at something like $40,000, increasing to full professorial salary – between $60,000 and $100,000 – if the writer receives tenure. That's good money, plus campuses have lawns and workout facilities and health insurance, and there are summer vacations during which the writer can earn extra as a counselor at one of those writing camps for adults.

On the minus side, he must attend departmental meetings and fight off departmental intrigues. Worse, he must teach workshop, which means responding intelligently and at length to manuscripts. A writer who ignores his teaching duties in favor of his own writing will spend an inordinate amount of time feeling guilty; one who scrupulously reads and comments on student manuscripts will have a clearer conscience. But he will be spending all his time with children.

Journalism's pitfalls are well known. Bad magazines vulgarize your ideas and literally spray your pages with cologne. Good magazines are even worse: they do style editing, copyediting, query editing, bullet-proofing – and as you emerge from the subway with your trash bag of books (a burnt offering to the fact-checker), you suddenly realize that you have landed a $6-an-hour job, featuring heavy lifting.

Yet the biggest pitfall of journalism is not penury but vanity. Your name is in print; it is even, perhaps, in print in the most august possible venue. But you are still serving someone else's idea of their readership – and their idea of you. You are still just doing journalism – or, worse, book reviewing. 'What lice will do, when they have no more blood to suck,' as the 19th century put it.

Odd jobs – usually copyediting, tutoring, Power-Point, graphic design; I don't know any writers who wait tables but probably some exist – seem like a better idea in terms of one's intellectual independence. But these can lead to a kind of desperation. What if your writing doesn't make it? How long can you keep this up? You have no social position outside the artistic community; you have limited funds; you call yourself a writer but your name does not appear anywhere in print. Worst of all, for every one of *you*, there are five or ten or fifteen others, also working on novels, who are just total fakers – they have to be, statistically speaking. Journalism at least binds you to the world of publishing in some palpable way; the odd jobs leave you indefinitely in exile. It would take a great deal of strength not to grow bitter under these circumstances, and demoralized. Your success, if it comes, might still come too late.

And then, of course, a writer can make money by publishing a book. But if it is depressing to lack social status and copyedit *Us Weekly*, it is even more depressing to talk about publishing – because *this* in fact is what you've worked for your entire life. Except now you will learn about the way of things. That book you wrote has sales figures to shoot for; it has a sales force to help it. And you are in debt. Publishers have always used anemic sales to bully their writers – Malcolm Cowley speaks of their claim that only after 10,000 copies sold could they break even; of course, says the good-natured Cowley, 'they may have been displaying a human weakness for exaggeration.' Now publishers come to lunch armed with Nielsen BookScan – to the same effect. The comical thing about this up-to-the-minute point-of-sale technology is how inaccurate everyone agrees it to be – '522 copies trade cloth' sold might mean 800 or 1,000 or 1,200 because so many bookstores don't participate. The less comical thing is that, as a measure of short-term popularity, it is all too accurate – *Everything Is Illuminated*, a work of Jewish kitsch, has sold, according to BookScan, 271,433 copies since it came out in 2002; meanwhile, Sam Lipsyte's *Home Land*, a scabrous work of Jewish humor, has sold 13,503 copies; Michael Walzer's *Arguing about War*, a work of political philosophy in the skeptical Jewish tradition, has sold 3,136. Of course one knew this; of course, one was not a fool; yet it's still hard to believe.

The very precision of the numbers numbs the publishers into a false sense of their finality. They cannot imagine a book good enough to have its sales in the future. Publishers wish things were otherwise, they will tell you; they would rather publish better books; *but the numbers don't lie.* The chief impression one gets of publishers these days is not of greed or corporatism but demoralization and confusion. They have acquired a manuscript; they know how they feel about it; they probably even know how reviewers will feel about it; but what about the public? Those people are animals. Over lunch the publisher tells his writer what it's like out there – 'You have no idea.' In fact the writer does have an idea: he lives 'out there.' But the publisher can't hear him; he is like an online poker player, always checking the computer. Nielsen BookScan rules.

'That equivocal figure,' Pierre Bourdieu calls the publisher, 'through whom the logic of the economy is brought to the heart of the sub-field of production.' Yes, but he's all the writer's got. Is he looking tired? Poor publisher – last week he became so discombobulated by the 'realities of the publishing industry' that he paid $400,000 for the first novel of a blogger. 'He'll be promoting the book on his blog!' the publisher tells his writer over seared ahi tuna. 'Which, you see, is read by *other bloggers*!' He is like Major McLaughlin, the cursed, hapless owner of the Chicago Blackhawks who once became so frustrated with his team's play, and successive coaches' failure to mend it, that he hired a man who'd sent him a letter about the team in the mail.

Once the book is published it only gets worse: the writer proceeds to the Cavalry of publicity. Advances on first books vary – about $20,000 to $60,000 for a book of stories, though sometimes higher; between

$50,000 and $250,000 for a 'literary' novel, though also, sometimes, higher. Even the top figure – $250,000 – which seems like so much, and *is* so much, still represents on both sides of the writing and rewriting, the pre-publication and post-publication, about four years of work – $60,000 a year, the same as a hack lifestyle journalist in New York. But the costs! The humiliations! No one will ever forgive a writer for getting so much money in one lump – not the press, not other writers, and his publisher least of all. He will make certain the phrase 'advance against royalties' is not forgotten, and insist the writer bleed and mortify himself to make it back.

Our forefathers the Puritans used to have, in addition to days of thanksgiving, 'days of humiliation,' when they prostrated themselves before God and begged for an end to their afflictions. 'Before long,' the intellectual historian Perry Miller wrote, 'it became apparent that there were more causes for humiliation than for rejoicing.' And so it is for the published author. The recent dress-down of James Frey and his publisher by Oprah was an event that people at publishing houses gathered to watch on their office televisions as if it were the *Challenger* disaster. But this was just karmic revenge on publishers and their authors, who spend every day prostituting themselves: with photographs, interviews, readings with accordions, live blogs on Amazon.com ('In the desert, it probably doesn't matter if the groundhog sees his shadow,' went a recent entry by the novelist Rick Moody, a man who for all his sins is still the author of *The Ice Storm*, and deserves better than this. 'Oh, by the way, the film *Groundhog Day* is one of my favorites!') Henry James complained about writers being dragooned into 'the periodical prattle about the future of fiction.' If only that were the worst of it. Consider the blurb: How humiliating that younger writers should spend so much time soliciting endorsements from more established writers, and how absurd that established writers should have to apologize for not providing them. If they'd wanted to be ad copywriters, they'd have done that, and been paid for it. But they once asked for those blurbs, too.

In the age of BookScan, only an unpublished writer is allowed to keep his dignity.

———

Most writers lived as before, on crumbs from a dozen different tables. Meanwhile a few dozen or even a hundred of the most popular writers were earning money about at the rate of war contractors.
  – Malcolm Cowley on the book-of-the-month club era, 1946

Not long ago I found a very interesting letter, a letter of advice, folded into one of my mother's old books. It was from the Russian émigré writer Sergei Dovlatov, to another writer, apparently newly arrived. My mother was a literary critic, but I don't know how that letter got into that book; in any case, it describes literary life here in the States – the two clashing editors of the émigré journals, in particular, one of whom is pleasant and never pays, while the other is unpleasant and does. And so on.

Dovlatov had done his Soviet army service as a guard in a labor camp and wrote dark, funny stories about camp life – 'Solzhenitsyn believes that the camps are hell,' he wrote, explaining the difference between himself and the master. 'Whereas I believe that hell is us.' In 1979, he emigrated to Forest Hills, Queens, and began writing about the Russians there. He published some stories in the *New Yorker*, met often with his good friend Joseph Brodsky, and died, mostly of alcoholism, at the age of 48. He had liked it here. 'America's an interesting place,' Dovlatov concluded in the letter that was folded, for some reason, into one of my mother's books. 'Eventually you find someone to publish you. And you earn some money. You even find a wife. Things work out.'

It's true. It's mostly true. And when you think of the long-standing idea of art in opposition to the dominant culture, if only by keeping its autonomy from the pursuit of money – the only common value great writers from right to left have acknowledged – you begin to sense what we have lost. Capitalism as a system for the equitable distribution of goods is troublesome enough; as a way of measuring success it is useless. When you begin to think the advances doled out to writers by major corporations possess anything but an accidental correlation to artistic worth, you are finished. Everything becomes publicity. How many writers now refuse to be photographed? How many refuse to sit for idiotic 'lifestyle' pieces? Or to write supplemental reading group 'guides' for their paperbacks? Everyone along the chain of production compromises a tiny bit and suddenly Jay McInerney is a guest judge on *Iron Chef*.

Publicity is not everything; money, also. Emile Zola was so concerned that he would lose his position in French artistic circles because of his incredible popularity that he formulated an aesthetic theory to explain his art. As recently as five years ago, Jonathan Franzen, too, worried lest his *Corrections* might seem to have fallen outside the main development of the American art novel, justified his work in aesthetic terms. (For doing so, for letting his guard down in public in tortured meditations on aesthetic value, Franzen has been made to pay, and pay again, by inferiors whose idea of good literature is German film.) Now writers simply point to their sales figures and accuse other writers of jealousy. Well, it's true. Everyone wants money, and needs it ('a woman must have money and a room of her own'). The only relevant question is what you are willing to do for it.

As for me and my $40,000, I recently went off contract at *New York* so I could finish a book of stories. My last article for the magazine, written as a freelancer, was about the New York Rangers. I received $7,000 – a lot. Two weeks later I hurt my finger playing football on a muddy field in Prospect Park.

Sitting in New York Methodist, my finger worrisomely bent and swollen, I watched a man in scrubs yell into his cell phone: '1.2 million! Yeah! We put down 400!' The doctor had bought a condo.

This was the hand surgeon. After glancing briefly at my X-rays, the surgeon declared I needed surgery.

'How about a splint?' I said.

'No way.'

I decided to negotiate. 'I can afford $3,000,' I said.

'I'm not a financial adviser.'

'Well, how much will it be?'

'$7,000.'

Ha ha. It was like an O. Henry story: I wrote the article, they fixed my finger.

Except it wasn't like that, because I declined the surgery and kept the money. At my current rate of spending, it will last me three months. That should be enough. I hope that's enough.

Wesley Yang

– The Face of Seung-Hui Cho –

T he first school shooter of the 1990s was an Asian
     boy who played the violin. I laughed when I
heard an account of the rampage from my friend Ethan
Gooding, who had survived it. Ethan forgave me my
reaction. I think he knew by then that most people,
facing up to a real atrocity, as opposed to the hundreds
they'd seen on TV, didn't know how to act.

Ethan had left New Providence High School in
central New Jersey for the progressive utopia of Simon's
Rock College of Bard in Great Barrington, Massachu-
setts. Simon's Rock was a school for high school jun-
iors and seniors ready for college-level work, a refuge
for brilliant misfits, wounded prodigies, and budding
homosexuals. Ethan was a pretty bright kid, brighter
than me, but mostly he was a budding homosexual.
One day in gym class at New Providence, Ethan made
a two-handed set shot from half-court using a kick-
ball while dressed in buttercup-yellow short-shorts
and earned the nickname 'Maurice.' This was not a
reference to E. M. Forster's frank novel of gay love,
but to Maurice Cheeks, the great Philadelphia 76ers
point guard. The unintended resonance was savored
by those few of us who could discern it. Ethan had

a striking pre-Raphaelite pallor set off against flaming red cheeks and lips with the puckered epicene aspect that speaking the French language too young will impart to a decent American mouth. None of this in itself meant, necessarily, that he was going to become gay, but then – well, he was.

Gay-bashing was less of a hate crime back then and more of a patriotic duty, particularly in a race-segregated, heavily Catholic suburb like New Providence. At Youth & Government, the YMCA-sponsored mock legislature attended by suck-ups with Napoleon complexes, the 'governor' from our school introduced a bill to 'build an island of garbage off of the Jersey Shore' where we could 'put all the homosexuals.' We all chortled along, none more loudly than the closet cases in our midst. It was the kind of place you wanted to flee so badly that you trained yourself to forget the impulse.

But then there was a place called New York, only a half hour's drive away. We made our first anxious forays into New York City nightlife, Ethan and I and Jasper Chung, the other Korean kid from my high school (himself a governor of the mock legislature, and also a closet homosexual). We tried to get into the back room of the Limelight, where the real party was happening. 'Try to look cute,' Ethan told me, brushing my hair with a concerned, appraising look. Then he sucked in his cheeks, which I guess was his way of looking cute, or at least making his face less round. It would be more than a decade and a half before I learned what a smile could do for you (it is one way to hold at bay the world's cruelty), so I made a fish-eyed grimace in emulation of David Gahan of Depeche Mode. They never let us into the back room.

Those were the wild Peter Gatien days, when the place was still bristling with drugs and prostitution, most of which managed to pass us by. But we were assailed by a phalanx of sweaty, shirtless Long Island beefcake. Ethan would, to my frightened astonishment, meet other guys, and go off into a dark corner with them, and leave me to fend for myself, which I was not equipped to do. I'd get dehydrated and wear an anxious scowl. I would attempt some rudimentary sociological and semiotic reading of the scene that swirled all around me. I couldn't relax.

Not that I was myself homosexual. True, my heterosexuality was notional. I wasn't much to look at (skinny, acne-prone, brace-faced, bespectacled, and Asian), and inasmuch as I was ugly, I also had a bad personality. While Ethan was easing himself into same-sex experimentation, I was learning about the torments and transports of misanthropy.

'That kid,' I remember overhearing one of the baseball players say, 'is a misfit.' No one ever shoved my head in a locker, the way they did the one amber-tinted Afghani kid, or P. J., the big dumb sweet slow kid, and nobody ever pelted me with rocks, as they did Doug Urbano, who was fat and working class (his father was a truck driver, and sometimes, when he lectured us about the vital role that truck drivers play in the American economy – they really do, you know – he was jeered). But these judgments stayed with me.

Jasper once told me that I was 'essentially unlovable.' I've always held that observation close to my heart, turning to it often. It's true of some people – that there's no reason anyone should love or care about them, because they aren't appealing on the outside, and that once you dig into the real person beneath the shell (if, for some obscure if not actively perverse reason, you bother), you find the real inner ugliness. I knew lots of people like that – unloved because unlovable. Toward them I was always cold. Maybe I held them at arm's length to disguise from myself our shared predicament. And so, by trying to disguise something from yourself, you declare it to everyone else – because part of what makes a person unlovable is his inability to love.

One day we were hanging out with Ethan in Jasper's room over winter break. Ethan was telling us all about Simon's Rock, and – this might be an invented memory; it feels real, yet I can't rely on it; the very feeling of reality makes me distrust it – Ethan told me that I reminded him of this weird Asian guy at his school, whom he then proceeded to describe. Ethan, cherubic complexion notwithstanding, could actually be pretty mean. He was proud of his ability to wound with a well-chosen phrase coined in an instant, which is not to say that I didn't aspire to the same facility. It's just that he really had it. In any case, Wayne, my double, was an Asian boy ill at ease in the world and he had a chip on his shoulder. His father had been an officer in the Taiwanese air force, and his mother had been a Suzuki-method violin teacher. For a time, Wayne had been among the best violinists in the world in his age group. He was headed along the familiar track of Asian American assimilation. By the time he arrived at Simon's Rock, he had other things to prove.

The gay guys liked to tease Wayne and intimate that he might be one of them. It was good-natured ribbing, gentle to the extent that it was not tinged with gay malice; and who could begrudge them their share of malice – a little or a lot – given the world they were entering? On top of everything else, an incurable illness spread by the kind of sex you were already having or else aching to have was killing off a whole generation of your predecessors. You could get a rise out of Wayne, and he deserved it: here he was at this place where people were finally free to be who they really were, and who he really was turned out to be someone who didn't want other people to be free to be who they were. He had fled Montana only to discover his continuing allegiance to its mores. And who knows, conceivably he was even a bit bi-curious. 'How tough are you?' Wayne's friends used to ask him, egging him on. 'I'm tough!' he would shout.

By now the story of Wayne Lo has been well told,

though he has not become a figure of American legend. (His certified authentic 'murderabilia' drawings were fetching just $7.50 on his website at the time his jailers shut it down.) On Monday, December 14, 1992, a package arrived for him in the mail from a North Carolina company called Classic Arms. It contained 200 rounds of ammunition that Wayne had ordered using his mother's credit card. The school's dean held the package, and, after questioning Wayne about what was inside it (Wayne assured him that it was a Christmas gift), gave it back to him. Liberals! They'll hand over the ammunition that their enemies will use to kill them.

Ethan told his version of the story to Jasper and me over hamburgers at the A&W Restaurant at the Short Hills Mall. Wayne had started hanging out with some other students who wanted to rebel against the orthodoxy of difference at Simon's Rock. They listened to Rush Limbaugh and joked about killing people. They were suspicious of Jews and blacks and homosexuals and . . . did they make an official exception for Asians? Wayne wrote a paper proposing a solution to the AIDS crisis: Kill them all. He lacked the imagination to come up with the island of garbage disposal. Then, according to psychiatrists hired by his defense, Wayne was overtaken by a 'somatic hallucination' – not heard, but directly experienced in his body – of God urging him to punish the sinners of Simon's Rock.

It was a more innocent time, in a way. The Berlin Wall had come down. Crime rates were beginning the historic fall they were to make during the 1990s. American soldiers were ensconced in the Persian Gulf, having recently kept the armies of Saddam Hussein from entering the land of the two holy places. People didn't know about school shooters back then. They still thought that Asian men were happy to be (as Ethan liked to call us) the Other White People. Or even, as many people were suggesting, the New Jews. And for the most part, Asian people were happy – and are. I mean, maybe they were nerds, maybe they were faceless drones, but did anybody know they were angry? What could they be angry about? They were getting rich with the rest of America – and reassuring everyone of our openness and our tolerance for everyone prepared to embrace the American dream.

Lo went around the campus with the Chinese-made SKS Carbine rifle that he bought in a neighboring town. He shot and killed two people and wounded four others. Had his rampage not ended prematurely when his rifle repeatedly jammed (cheap Chinese junk), he might have set a record that no one was going to best. Instead, he called the police and negotiated his surrender.

The perpetrator of the largest mass murder in American history was an Asian boy who wrote poems, short stories, a novel, and plays. I gazed at the sad blank mug of Seung-Hui Cho staring out at the world on CNN.com – the face-forward shot that was all the press had before they received Cho's multimedia

50

manifesto, mailed on the day of the shootings, with its ghastly autoerotic glamour shots (Cho pointing gun at camera; Cho with a hammer; Cho pointing gun at his head). I felt, looking at the photo, a very personal revulsion. Millions of others reviled this person, but my own loathing was more intimate. Those lugubrious eyes, that elongated face behind wire-frame glasses: He looks like me, I thought.

This was another inappropriate reaction. But the photo leapt out at me at a funny time in my life. I had come to New York five years earlier, to create a life for myself there. I had not created a life for myself there. I had wanted to find the emerging writers and thinkers of my generation. I had found the sycophants, careerists, and media parasites who were redefining mediocrity for the 21st century. I had wanted to remain true to myself as a writer, and also to succeed; I wanted to be courageous and merciless in defense of the downtrodden, and I wanted to be celebrated for it. This was a naïve and puerile desire and one that could not be realized – at least not by me, not in this world. It could not be done without a facility (and a taste) for ingratiation that I lacked. It could not be done without first occupying a position of strength and privilege that I did not command – because, as Jesus said, to him who hath, more will be given; nor without being enterprising and calculating in a way that I wasn't – because, as Jesus went on to say, to him who hath not, even that which he hath will be taken from him. It seemed to me that every kind of life, and even the extinction of life, was preferable to the one that I was living, which is not to say I had the strength either to change my life, or to end it.

And then to be confronted by that face. Because physiognomy is a powerful thing. It establishes identification and aversion, and all the more so in an age that is officially color-blind. Such impulses operate beneath the gaze of the supervisory intelligence, at a visceral level that may be the most honest part of us. You see a face that looks like yours.

You know that there's an existential knowledge you have in common with that face. Both of you know what it's like to have a cultural code superimposed atop your face, and if it's a code that abashes, nullifies, and unmans you, then you confront every visible reflection of that code with a feeling of mingled curiosity and wariness. When I'm out by myself in the city – at the movies or at a restaurant – I'll often see other Asian men out by themselves in the city. We can't even look at each other for the strange vertigo we induce in one another.

Let's talk about legible faces. You know those short, brown-toned South American immigrants that pick your fruit, slaughter your meat, and bus your tables? Would you – a respectable person with a middle-class upbringing – ever consider going on a date with one of them? It's a rude question, because it affects to inquire into what everyone gets to know at the cost of forever leaving it unspoken. But if you were to put your unspoken thoughts into words, they might sound something like this: Not only are these people busing the tables, slaughtering the meat, and picking the fruit, they are the descendants of the people who bused the tables, slaughtered the meat, and picked the fruit of the Aztecs and Incas. The Spanish colonizers slaughtered or mixed their blood with the princes, priests, scholars, artisans, warriors, and beautiful women of the indigenous Americas, leaving untouched a class of Morlocks bred for good-natured servility and thus now tailor-made to the demands of an increasingly feudal postindustrial America. That's, by the way, part of the emotional undertow of the immigration debate, the thing that makes an honest appraisal of the issue impossible, because you can never put anything right without first admitting you're in the wrong.

So: Seung-Hui Cho's face. A perfectly unremarkable Korean face – beady-eyed, brown-toned, a small plump-lipped mouth, eyebrows high off his eyelids, with crooked glasses perched on his nose. It's not an ugly face, exactly; it's not a badly made face. It's just a face that has nothing to do with the desires of women in this country. It's a face belonging to a person who, if he were emailing you, or sending you instant messages, and you were a normal, happy, healthy American girl at an upper second-tier American university – and that's what Cho was doing in the fall of 2005, emailing and writing instant messages to girls – you would consider reporting it to campus security. Which is what they did, the girls who were contacted by Cho.

First, you imagine, they tried to dissuade him in the usual way. You try to be polite, but also to suggest that you'd actually prefer that your correspondent, if he could, you know, maybe – oh, I don't know – Disappear from your life forever? How about that? – and you had to do this subtly enough not to implicate yourself in anything damaging to your own self-image as a nice person, but then not so subtly that your correspondent would miss the point. When Cho missed the point, the girls had to call the campus police. They did not want him arrested, and they did not press charges. They just had to make clear that while Cho thought he was having one kind of encounter (a potentially romantic one), he was in fact having another kind of encounter (a potentially criminal one), and to show him that the state would intervene on their behalf if he couldn't come to terms with this reality. And so, the police didn't press any charges, but they did have a man-to-man talk with Cho, and conveyed to him the message that it would be better if he cut it out.

Seung-Hui Cho's is the kind of face for which the appropriate response to an expression of longing or need involves armed guards. I am not questioning the choices that these girls made; I am affirming those choices. But I'm talking about the Cho that existed before anyone was killed by him – the one who showed proficiency in beer pong at the one fraternity party his roommates took him to, and who told his roommates he had a girlfriend named Jelly who was a supermodel from outer space; who called one of his roommates to tell him that he had been on vacation with Vladimir Putin; and who emailed Lucinda Roy, director of the Creative Writing program, seeking guidance about how to submit his novel to publishers. 'My novel is relatively short,' he wrote. 'It's sort of like Tom Sawyer, except that it's really silly or pathetic, depending on how you look at it.'

Of course, there are a lot of things that Cho might have done to change his social fortunes that he declined to do. Either out of incompetence, stubbornness, or plain old bat-shit craziness, Cho missed many boats that might have ferried him away from his dark fate. For one, he could have dressed a little bit better. He might have tried to do something with his hair. Being a little less bat-shit crazy couldn't have hurt.

Above all, he could have cultivated his taste in music. He was 'obsessed with downloading music from the Internet,' the press reported, putting a sinister cast on something that everyone of a certain age does. But the song he continually played on his laptop, driving his roommates to distraction, wasn't some nihilistic rhapsody of wasted youth. It wasn't Trent Reznor of Nine Inch Nails saying he wanted to fuck you like an animal, and it wasn't the thick lugubrious whine of James Hetfield of Metallica declaring that what he'd felt, and what he'd known, never shone through in what he'd shown.

No, it was the cruddiest, most generic grunge-rock anthem of the '90s, Collective Soul's 'Shine.' 'Shine' came out in 1994, and you only had to hear the first minute to know that whatever was truly unyielding about the music Nirvana spawned by breaking punk into the mainstream was already finished. The song cynically mouths 'life-affirming' clichés noxious to the spirit of punk rock, but then these are not, given the situation, without their own pathos. You could picture the Cho who stalked around campus not saying a word to anyone, even when a classmate offered him money to speak, coming home in silence to listen to these lyrics repeat in an infinite loop on his laptop, and even, one day, to write them on his wall:

Teach me how to speak
Teach me how to share
Teach me where to go
Tell me will love be there (love be there)
Whoa-oh-oh-oh, heaven let your light shine down.

'You were the single biggest dork school shooter of all time,' opined one internet chat board participant, and it was hard to disagree. Cho was so disaffected that he couldn't even get the symbols of disaffection right. In the fall of 2005, when he made the mistake of instant-messaging girls, Cho was also attending Nikki Giovanni's large creative writing class. He would wear reflector glasses with a baseball cap obscuring his face.

Giovanni, who believed that openness was vital to the goals of the class, stood by his desk at the beginning of each session to make him take off the disguise. He later began showing up with a scarf wrapped around his head, 'Bedouin-style,' as Giovanni put it. When the attendance sheet was passed around, he signed his name as a question mark.

The class set Cho off, somehow – maybe because he had enrolled in the hope that his genius would be recognized, and it was not recognized. He began snapping pictures of female classmates with his cellphone camera from underneath his desk. Eventually, many of the seventy students enrolled in the class stopped coming. That's when Giovanni went to Lucinda Roy and insisted that Cho be barred from her workshop. She refused, in the words of one article about it, to be 'bullied' by Cho.

'He was writing, just weird things,' Giovanni told the *New York Times*. 'I don't know if I'm allowed to say what he was writing about. . . . He was writing poetry, it was terrible, it was not like poetry, it was intimidating.' Giovanni's personal website has a list of all her honors and awards and another page for all the honorary degrees she has earned – nineteen since 1972 – and a brief biography that identifies her as 'a world-renowned poet, writer, commentator, activist, and educator,' whose 'outspokenness, in her writing and in lectures, has brought the eyes of the world upon her.' Oprah Winfrey has named her one of her twenty-five living legends. 'We are sad today, and we will be sad for quite a while,' the 63-year-old eminence told the convocation to mourn Seung-Hui Cho's victims. 'We are not moving on, we are embracing our mourning.'

It's a perfectly consistent picture: Giovanni the winner of awards, and Giovanni the wise and grand-motherly presence on Oprah. But if you knew more about the writing of Nikki Giovanni, you couldn't help but wonder two things. What would the Nikki Giovanni of 2007 have made of a poem published by the Nikki Giovanni of 1968, and what would the Nikki Giovanni of 1968 have made of the Nikki Giovanni of the present? The Nikki Giovanni of 1968 wrote this:

Nigger
Can you kill
Can you kill
Can a nigger kill
Can a nigger kill a honkie
Can a nigger kill the Man
Can you kill nigger
Huh? nigger can you kill
Do you know how to draw blood
Can you poison
Can you stab-a-Jew
Can you kill huh? nigger
Can you kill

Back then Giovanni was writing about a race war that seemed like it really might break out at home, even as the country was fighting what she saw as an imperialist war in Vietnam. Black militancy was something that many people admired, and many more felt sympathy toward, given the brutal history of enslavement, rape, terrorism, disenfranchisement, lynching, and segregation that blacks had endured in this country.

And so you wonder what would have happened if, for instance, Cho's poems (and thoughts) had found a way to connect his pain to his ethnic identity. Would Giovanni have been less intimidated if she could have understood Cho as an aggrieved Asian man, instead of an aggrieved man who happened to be Asian? Or if he were black and wrote the way he did? Or if he were Palestinian and managed to tie his violent grievances to a real political conflict existing in the world? (Can you bomb-a-Jew?) Giovanni knows black rage, and she knows the source of women's bitterness. We all do. We know gay pride. We know, in short, identity politics, which, when it isn't acting as a violent outlet for the narcissism of the age, can serve as its antidote, binding people into imagined collectivities capable of taking action to secure their interests and assert their personhood.

Cho did not think of himself as Asian; he did not think of himself ethnically at all. He was a pimply friendless suburban teenager whom no woman would want to have sex with: that's what he was. And it turned out that in his imagination he was a warrior on behalf of every lonely invisible human being in America. This was his ghastly, insane mistake. This is what we learned from the speech Cho gave in the video he mailed to NBC News. For Cho, the cause to fight for is 'the dorky kid that [you] publicly humiliated and spat on,' whom you treated like 'a filthy street dog' and an 'ugly, little, retarded, low-life kid' – not just Cho, not just his solitary narcissistic frenzy, but also that of his 'children,' his 'brothers and sisters' – an imagined community of losers who would leave behind their status as outcasts from the American consensus and attain the dignity of warriors – by killing innocent civilians.

Cho enclosed his speech, too, in the NBC packet, as 'writings.'

You had everything you wanted. Your Mercedes wasn't enough, you brats, your golden necklaces weren't enough, you snobs, your trust fund wasn't enough . . .

You have vandalized my heart, raped my soul and torched my conscience. You thought it was one pathetic, bored life you were extinguishing.

I die like Jesus Christ, to inspire generations of the weak and defenseless people.

Cho imagines the one thing that can never exist – the coming to consciousness and the joining in solidarity of the modern class of losers. Though his soft Asian face could only have been a hindrance to him, Cho did not perceive his pain as stemming from being Asian: he did not perceive himself in a world of identity politics, of groups and fragments of groups, of groups oppressing and fighting other groups. Cho's world is a world of individually determined fortunes, of winners and losers in the marketplace of status, cash, and expression. Cho sees a system of social competition that renders some people absolutely immiserated while others grow obscenely rich.

When I was at Rutgers I knew a guy named Samuel Goldfarb. Samuel was prematurely middle-aged, not just in his dimensions, which were bloated, and not just in his complexion, which was pale but flushed with the exertion of holding himself upright – sweat would dapple the groove between his upper lip and nose – but above all in something he exuded, which was a pheromone of loneliness and hostility. Samuel had gone off to Reed College, and, after a couple of years of feeling alienated in that liberal utopia, he had returned east. Samuel was one of the students at Rutgers who was clearly more intellectually sophisticated than I. He knew more, he had read more, and it showed. He was the kind of nominal left-winger who admired the works of Carl Schmitt before many others had gotten onto that trend, and he knew all about the Frankfurt School, and he was already jaded about the postmodernists when others were still enraptured by the discovery of them. In addition to being the kind of leftist who read a Nazi legal theorist to be contrarian, Samuel was also the kind of aspiring academic so contemptuous of the postmodern academy that he was likely to go into investment banking and make pots of money while jeering at the rest of humanity, because that was so much more punk rock than any other alternative to it. He identified his 'lifestyle' – and of course he put that word into derisive quote marks when he used it – as 'indie rock,' but Samuel's irony had extra bite to it, real cruelty and rancor, that was tonally off-kilter for the indie rock scene, which, as it manifested itself at Rutgers, was taciturn to the point of autism, passive-aggressive, and anti-intellectual, but far too cool and subdued for the exertions of overt cruelty.

You saw a look of sadness and yearning in Samuel's face when he had subsided from one of his misanthropic tirades – there was no limit to the scorn he heaped on the intellectual pretensions of others – and it put you on guard against him. What you sensed about him was that his abiding rage was closely linked to the fact that he was fat and ugly in a uniquely unappealing way, and that this compounded with his unappealing rage made him the sort of person that no woman would ever want to touch. He seemed arrayed in that wild rancor that sexual frustration can bestow on a man, and everything about his persona – his coruscating irony, his unbelievable intellectual snobbery – seemed a way to channel and thus defend himself against this consuming bitterness. He was ugly on the outside and once you got past that you found the true ugliness on the inside.

And then below that ugliness you found a vulnerable person who desperately needed to be seen and touched and known as a human phenomenon. And above all, you wanted nothing to do with that, because once you touched the source of his loneliness, there would be no end to it, and even if you took it upon yourself to appease this unappeasable need, he would eventually decide to revenge himself against a world that had held him at bay, and there would be no better target for this revenge than you, precisely because you were the person who'd dared to draw the nearest. This is what you felt instantly, without having to put it into words (it's what I felt, anyway, though it might have been pure projection), the moment you met Samuel. For all that he could be amusing to talk to, and for all that he was visibly a nice guy despite all I've just said, you were careful to keep your distance.

Samuel used to complain about declining academic standards. He said that without much work he was acing all of his classes. This was a way of exalting himself slightly while mostly denigrating others, which made it an exemplary statement of his, but it was also a suspect statement, since no one had asked. One day, while I was in the history department's front office, I noticed a plastic crate full of hanging folders. In one of those folders, I found my own academic transcript in its entirety. Then I looked for Samuel's. Like mine, it was riddled with Ds and Fs. And while what Samuel had said about academic standards and his own aptitude was surely true, it was also true that he had lied – and I suppose I understand why. If your only claim to self-respect was your intellectual superiority, and you had more or less flunked out of Reed College because of the crushing loneliness and depression you encountered once you realized that liberal utopia wasn't going to embrace you as it did the willowy, stylish high school outcasts who surrounded you – and if your grades weren't much better at Rutgers (a pathetic public university, even though you hated Reed more), you might be forced to lie about those grades, because they were the public face of all you had left – your intellectual superiority – and even after all you'd endured, or maybe because of it, your public face still mattered. Unaware that the contrary evidence was there for anyone to check (it should not have been) or that a person inclined to check it existed (I should not have looked), you would assume that you could tell this lie without being caught.

I mentioned this incident to a mutual acquaintance, who proceeded to tell Samuel, who accused me of making up lies about him, and turned me into the great enemy of his life – he was clearly looking for one – which was too bad and a little disconcerting, because, as I explained to him, he and his grades had never meant anything to me. And yet I had only read two transcripts, his and mine, mostly because I suspected, correctly, that he was telling lies. Samuel had been wronged by me, and it would have been right for me to apologize, but I had some hostility of my own, so instead I told him that he was ugly on the outside, but even uglier on the inside, and that he meant nothing to me, and his enmity counted for nothing to me. And this was true. I had recognized him as a person with whom I had some mutual understanding – overlapping interests and, most of all, overlapping pretensions – but I never wanted him as a friend. The image this whole affair calls up is the scene in *Born on the Fourth of July* in which two paraplegics in wheelchairs start wrestling around in anger, and then tip each other into a ditch by the side of the road, and fall out of their wheelchairs, and roll around on the ground in the dirt, from which they are unable to lift themselves.

I saw Samuel Goldfarb at a coffee shop near Union Square about a year ago. He was chatting up the Eastern European counter girls. You could tell that he was a regular. He had put on a lot of weight and lost more of his hair, and his skin had lost none of its sebaceous excess. He had really become, at 32 or 33, the ruined middle-aged man that he already seemed on the cusp of becoming in youth. He seemed like a nice, harmless guy, but then you could still discern loneliness and sexual desperation clinging to him, though it had lost some of its virulence. I was glad to see his resignation. And I knew that he was probably very rich, and I felt weirdly good on his behalf to know that if he had to be lonely, if he had to be one of the millions of sexually null men in America – and for all I knew, he could have studied the Game and become a world-class seducer in the intervening years, though it seemed unlikely ('Hey guys – quick question for you – do you believe in magic spells?' – I couldn't see it) – at least he could be rich.

Lack of money had taught me the value of money. I had learned that when I didn't have it – and by this I mean, really having none of it, as in, like, nothing, which was most of the time – I would become extremely unhappy. And that when I did have it, even a little bit of it, which was rare, my despondency was assuaged, and I became like a dry and dwindling houseplant that would rally and surge up from out of its dolor when watered. I deduced from this pattern that what I needed to do was find an occupation that would pay me a salary – it was amazing to think how long I had gone without one – and then I would have money all the time, and then I would be, if not happy, at least OK. And to come to this realization seemed a little bit like the moment in *1984* when Winston Smith decides that he loves Big Brother, but then even more than that it just felt like growing up and it felt like life. And so I figured that Samuel was fine; and while I was very far from fine, I thought someday I'd catch on to something and I'd eventually be fine too.

And maybe I still will, at that.

A friend of mine wrote a book about online dating. She talked to hundreds of people about their experiences. Online, you become the person you've always known yourself to be, deep down. Online, you're explicit about the fact that you are paying for a service, and you're explicit about the fact that what you're paying for is to get what you really want, and what you're paying for is the ability to remove that annoying bit of residual romantic nonsense that gets us into annoying situations in life where we have to face up to the fact that we are rational profit maximizers in nothing so much as those intimate areas where we pretend to be otherwise. And so, people on the dating sites disclose what they really want, and also what they really don't want.

This friend talked to one man from Maryland who put up his profile on Match.com one night a few years back. This man had good reason to think he would do well on the site. He made more than $150,000 a year; he was white; he was over six feet tall. The next morning, he woke up and checked his account. Over the course of the previous night, he had gotten many responses. How many responses had he gotten? How well could he expect to do, being a man able to check off, without lying, boxes that certified that he made more than $150,000 a year, that he was six feet four inches tall, and that he was white? How well do you think he was going to do on that site where people disclosed what they really wanted out of life and also what they really didn't want?

He had gotten six thousand responses in one night. The fact was that if there was something intriguing or beautiful about that man – and there's something beautiful about us all, if you look deeply enough – someone was going to take the trouble to find it out, and they'd love him for that thing, not because he was six feet four inches tall, and not because he made more than $150,000 a year. You'd find out about his love of truth and poetry, to the extent that it existed, or at least his ability to make you laugh, or his own ability to laugh at things that made you laugh too – things on TV. You could watch TV together. Because the thing you wanted to do was to find true love and have that true love coincide with everything else that you wanted from life, so that you could have all the benefits of one kind of ease, and all the moral credit that others had to win by forgoing that kind of ease (but you could have it all, so why not?), and so you were going to put yourself in a position to do that. And you weren't going to answer the ads of anyone with beady lugubrious eyes in a forlorn, brown-tinted face, and if that person wrote you a message, you weren't going to write him back, and you'd probably even, if it seemed like it was necessary, block all further emails from that person. And you'd be right to do that. You'd be behaving in the way that any rational person in your situation would behave. We all agree that the rational thing to do is to shut every trace of that person's existence out of your view. The question, though, is – what if it's not you shutting out the losers? What if you're the loser whom everyone is shutting out? Of course, every loser is shutting out an even more wretched loser. But what if, as far as you know, you're the lowest person at the low end of this hierarchy? What is your rational move then?

You wake to find yourself one of the disadvantaged of the fully liberated sexual marketplace. If you are a woman, maybe you notice that men have a habit of using and discarding you, pleading their own inconstancy and premature emotional debauchery as a sop to your wounded feelings. If you are a man, maybe you notice that the women who have been used and discarded by other, more highly valued men are happy to restore (for a while) their own broken self-esteem by stepping on you while you are prone, and reminding you that even a society of outcasts has its hierarchies. Indeed, these hierarchies are policed all the more ruthlessly the closer to the bottom you go.

For these people, we have nothing but options. Therapy, selective serotonin reuptake inhibitors, alcoholism, drug addiction, pornography, training in mixed martial arts, mail-order brides from former Soviet republics, sex tours in Southeast Asia, prostitution, video-game consoles, protein shakes and weight-lifting regimens, New Age medicine, obsession with pets or home furnishings, the recovery movement – all of which are modes of survival as opposed to forms of life. Each of these options compensates for a thing, love, that no person can flourish without, and each, in a different way, offers an endlessly deferred resolution to a conundrum that is effectively irresolvable. You could even say that our culture feeds off the plight of the poor in spirit in order to create new dependencies. You might even dare to say that an undernourished human soul – desperate and flailing, prone to seeking voluntary slavery in the midst of freedom and prosperity – is so conducive to the creation of new markets that it is itself the indispensable product of our culture and our time, at once its precondition and its goal.

There's a familiar narrative we all know about high school losers. It's the narrative of smart sitcoms and even edgy indie films. The high school loser grows up, fills out, goes to Brown or RISD, and becomes the ideal guy for every smart, sensitive, quirky-but-cute girl with glasses (who is, in turn, the female version of the loser made good). The traits that hindered him (or her) in one phase of life turn out to be a blessing in another, more enlightened phase, or else get cast aside. For many people, this is an accurate description of their experience – it is the experience of the writers and producers of these stories.

In the indie film version of Seung-Hui Cho's life, the escort Cho hired a few weeks before his massacre wouldn't have danced for him for fifteen minutes in a motel room and then shoved him away when he tried to touch her. Not every one of the girls he tried to talk to would have recoiled in horror from him. Something would have happened in that film to remind him, and us, of his incipient humanity – that horribly menaced and misshapen thing. He would have found a good-hearted person who had perhaps been touched in some way by the same hysteria – and don't we all know something about it? – that had consumed Cho's soul.

And this good-hearted girl or boy would have known how to forgive Cho for what he couldn't forgive himself – the unbearable, all-consuming shame of being ugly, weak, sick, poor, clumsy, and ungifted.

We know that Cho had dreamt of this indie film ending. He had been dreaming of it for a long time. In the spring semester of 2006, he wrote a story about a boy estranged from his classmates: 'Everyone is smiling and laughing as if they're in heaven-on-earth, something magical and enchanting about all the people's intrinsic nature that Bud will never experience.' But eventually the boy meets a 'Gothic Girl,' to whom he breaks down and confesses, 'I'm nothing. I'm a loser. I can't do anything. I was going to kill every god damn person in this damn school, swear to god I was, but I . . . couldn't. I just couldn't.'

Cho's short story about the Gothic Girl should have ended, but did not, with this declaration. Instead, he and the girl steal a car and drive to her house, where she retrieves 'a .8 caliber automatic rifle and a M16 machine gun,' and the story concludes when she tells the narrator, 'You and me. We can fight to claim our deserving throne.'

In real life, there was no Gothic Girl, no me to Cho's you, no other willing actors – whether sympathetic, heroic, or equally violently deranged – to populate the self-made movie of his life.

Having failed to make it as a novelist – he really did send a book proposal to a New York publisher –

Cho decided to make a film. This was a familiar trajectory, with a twist. He was going to collaborate with all the major television networks on it. In the days before his date with a self-appointed destiny, Cho was spotted working out in the college gym. He wanted his scrawny arms and chest to appear more credibly menacing than they were. How many of those men working their arms to the point of exhaustion were driven by the vain notion that they could improve their sexual prospects in the process? Cho had no such illusions. He was preparing a spectacle for the world to witness on TV, and he needed to look the part.

Carla Blumenkranz

– In Search of Gawker –

N ew York gossip website Gawker was launched
in 2002 by an internet entrepreneur and a naïf
new to the city – Professor Henry Higgins and his
Eliza Doolittle. Founder Nick Denton, a former *Financial Times* reporter, had helped start the early social
networking site First Tuesday, which arranged for web
and media entrepreneurs to go for drinks together.
Elizabeth Spiers, the 25-year-old writer he hired, was a
recent New York arrival who had kept a blog about her
life in finance. It's hard to believe that at first Gawker,
which we now know for 'knowing everything' about local media and celebrity culture, didn't even know what
to read. But in her very first posts (from March 2002),
Spiers writes blurbs to herself about what she's read or
should be reading. Flavorpill.com is 'cultural stimuli in
New York'; *New York* is a 'fluffy, bitchy city magazine';
and the *New York Observer* is 'the print inspiration for
Gawker, a pinkpaged broadsheet designed for the Upper East Side elite.'

Lists like this usually only exist in the notebooks
of young people who come to the city intent on figur-
ing it out. Spiers, who grew up in Alabama, attended
Duke, and then started her career in San Francisco,

made her notebooks public. She was not bored by any piece of information about New York. In her first few months as Gawker, she showed a disarming interest in maps of Manhattan (one, for instance, identified all the WiFi access points); she linked to *New Yorker* pieces she liked; and she strenuously objected to an alleged Tupperware party trend, as reported in the *Times* Style section. 'Please tell me this Tupperware thing is intentionally ironic so I can stop banging my head against the wall and screaming,' she wrote. Spiers, who was from a small town and probably knew from Tupperware, couldn't seem to stand the idea that, in the city, you might not get to throw everything away.

To a reader who first met Gawker a few years later, it can be surprising to read these posts, which combine the excitement and the put-on knowingness of a genuine novice. 'I think it's actually easier to write about Manhattan if you're an outsider,' Spiers explained on the site in March 2002. 'The absurdities, in particular, are much more apparent. The darker Manhattan-centric themes – class warfare as a recreational sport; pathological status obsession; and the complete, total, and wholly unapologetic embrace of decadence – are much more fascinating to us. [Ed. note – We can spend entire minutes thinking about them.]' This is the Spiers signature: the outburst of enthusiasm, followed by the well-timed, half-apologetic reversal. Sometimes she forgot the kicker and just told readers what a good time she was having. In one of her first pieces of media commentary, Spiers attended a 'New York media party,' for *Slate* magazine and new editor Jacob Weisberg. Spiers tried to dish some dirt: 'Everybody hates *Wired*'s Chris Anderson except for James Truman and Si Newhouse.' But that, it turned out, was a joke: 'Most people who know Anderson think he's a smart and charming guy.' Really, Spiers admitted, 'I have to gush': 'New York media people are witty, and that isn't a word I've used in a while.' The only problem was that Spiers's escort, in town from San Francisco, was exhausted by the end of it.

This couldn't last forever, of course – not everyone in New York was so nice and smart. After about six months, Spiers's focus shifted from what it was like to be a New Yorker trying to fill space in a new medium, the media blog (sitting at home reading Craigslist, compulsively checking Site Meter, finally leaving the house only to get her finger stuck in an ATM), to how the rest of the New York media worked. Spiers was straightforward about her desire to land a magazine job someday, and now she turned her attention to the mechanics of print publications. Gawker's official launch came in December 2002. No one got more notice on the site after that than former *Talk* and *New Yorker* editor Tina Brown, who had recently started her short-lived *Washington Post* media column, and Anna Wintour, the famous editor of *Vogue*.

Spiers meticulously cited mentions of Brown by better-situated gossip sources and gleefully quoted from her columns. (Brown was starting a TV talk show and worried that she'd lose her effectiveness as a journalist if she could no longer be a 'furtive, watchful presence in a low-cut sweater.' To which Spiers replied: 'The low-cut sweater, at least, works.') For Wintour, Spiers enlisted Condé Nast assistants to report on what the *Vogue* editor wore in the elevator ('sunglasses'), ordered at Starbucks (an apple fritter), and did to the hamburger guy at the cafeteria (fired him). Spiers hoped to cut these women down to her own size; at the same time, she was curious about how they got to be where they were. She felt no solidarity with Lauren Weisberger, author of the fictionalized *Vogue* exposé *The Devil Wears Prada*. Both young women, it seems clear, believed they had more to learn from Wintour than they did from each other. So Spiers dismissed Weisberger as quickly as possible: 'How naive do you have to be to sign up to work for Anna Wintour, expecting that she's going to be nice to you?'

Reading through the early Gawker archives means watching Spiers receive and record her New York education. As she began to notice, she could make herself a winning protagonist. Spiers worried theatrically that she had become too mean. She also started to write not only about what she saw but also what she wore, as though she were the heroine in the sitcom she and her readers could imagine of their upwardly mobile lives. That spring, she wrote a 1,500-word episode in which she sneaked into the Condé Nast cafeteria. Spiers dis-

guised herself (in 'a wrap dress and "fuck me" boots')
as a magazine assistant. Still – she pretended to be
vexed – she believed she had been recognized by 'a
Condé Nast executive.' As what – a feared gossip,
or an interviewee? It was getting hard to tell. Spiers,
who with increasing awareness played the role of the
bright-eyed careerist, was making a career out of that
persona.

Only a few months after its official launch, Gawker
was already a media industry phenomenon of some im-
portance. By May 2003, Denton reported on Gawker
that the site received more than 20,000 visitors per day
and 500,000 page views per month. This wasn't much
compared to the most successful competition (Slate.
com was reported to receive about 6 million visitors per
month), but it did speak to Gawker's sudden promi-
nence within, as the Daily News put it, 'chic Manhattan.' A *Times* profile soon placed Spiers at the center
of a 'New York School of bloggers.' She was the author
of 'tart prose' who started Gawker 'as a first step toward a writing career.' Obviously, it had worked, and
now she entered the awkward position of a careerist
who had mocked careerists, being mocked by other
anti-careerist careerists. In response to the *Times* article, Bullymag.com accused Spiers of 'the most cynical shallowness' – 'the kind that announces itself as
"honesty"' – and predicted that within two years the
scourge of the media world would be writing for *New
York* and *Radar*. To this Spiers responded that, in fact,

she would 'sell out much quicker.' Four months after the *Times* article, she left Gawker for *New York*.

After Spiers left, Denton is reported to have said that he feared readers would abandon Gawker. It certainly would have been strange to find another Elizabeth Spiers and have her start at the beginning. As it happened, Denton replaced Spiers with Choire Sicha, a young art dealer who had written for *New York* and gay culture sites years before Gawker started. Sicha was from Chicago and had not gone to college; he had lived on his own in San Francisco and New York for about a decade. Sicha was only a year older than Spiers but, unlike his predecessor, he wrote from a perspective that no longer betrayed any aspirations. His inclination from the start seems to have been, if not to write like a reporter, then to undertake the same erasure of perspective. Spiers had played a very smart straight girl to the New York media and her persona was part of her appeal. Sicha's own appeal was in being almost impersonally sharp and cruel and correct.

The transition from Spiers to Sicha came at a moment when Gawker was evolving from a single successful experiment to a chain of sites. Denton had launched Gizmodo (gadgets) and Fleshbot (pornography) in 2002 and 2003; in 2004, he started Wonkette (DC), Defamer (Hollywood), and Kinja (meta-blog). The purpose of these sites, from Denton's perspective, was to yield viewer numbers that would sell advertisements.

When Sicha became editor in August 2004, Gawker still didn't generate much ad revenue (about $2,000 per month, according to Denton, who posted the figure on his blog), but its viewer counts continued to rise. In November, Denton updated the site statistics: Gawker now received 30,000 visitors per day and over one million page views per month, twice the number he had reported only six months earlier.

If Gawker Media, as Denton called his business, could no longer market itself as an upstart, then neither could its flagship site. Sicha's perspective was hard to define but, from his first weeks at Gawker, he seemed both complicit with and distrustful of the milieu he described. His voice was often on the verge of dissolving into his material. Like a Method gossip, Sicha had a natural fluency in spin and slipped almost lyrically into the voices of the subjects he intended to critique. When he felt that these subjects, out of restraint or lack of imagination, hadn't pushed their blurbs far enough, Sicha obligingly did it for them. For one last *Sex & the City* ad campaign, he helpfully revised the slogan – 'Sex this good can't last forever' – for the Gawker set: 'Sooner or later they climb off you when they're done fucking you.' With more powerful people, his commentary seemed less conflicted, but still Sicha meticulously limited himself to their language. (*Paris Review* editor Brigid Hughes cheerfully insisted that the magazine was open to all prospective writers; Sicha gave 'the delightful Ms. Hughes a D for Disingenuous!') At

times his insults and his humor, in the language he imi-
tated, were so subtly placed that they could be missed
completely. His response to the publicist for Lauren
Weisberger, formerly Elizabeth Spiers's bête noire,
who was then promoting Weisberger's second novel,
simply mirrored the publicist's tone. Sicha confided:
'We'll be watching this one closely.'

If Sicha's wit could be discreet to the vanishing
point, his cruelty was also tamed by personal reti-
cence. His default style was informed and often ob-
scene but left few traces of the author. Even when
Sicha described places he had been, it was hard to
imagine him as other than a spectral figure. He listened to talk in bathrooms and elevators. He took
photos through the windows of the Maritime Hotel.
When speaking of himself, he mostly used 'we,' which
seemed more ambiguous than pseudo-grandiose, and
he noted his own vagueness when admitting overheard
conversations were 'paraphrased due to inattention.'
The few times Sicha wrote directly about his life, it
usually was couched as a journalistic ethics disclosure.
Twice Sicha published longer posts about Dale Peck,
a talented novelist who had become notorious for his
'hatchet job' book reviews in the *New Republic*. Both
times (the second because Stanley Crouch had slapped
Peck at a downtown restaurant), Sicha inhabited the
role of the journalist with the same careful humor as he
had inhabited the role of the publicist, parenthetically
noting that he and Peck had shared an apartment for

years: '[Full disclosure: Dale Peck and I share an Air-port network, and before WiFi, a DSL line, and before DSL, a dial-up connection.]'

Sicha's persona did not change much during his time at Gawker, but he did reveal himself to be invest-ed, in a strange way, in the integrity of Gawker as an in-stitution. One of the most extended stories he followed involved unprecedented self-revelation: the drama of his removal from Soho House, a private downtown club for media and arts-related professionals. Toward the end of his Gawker tenure, Sicha was asked not to renew his membership after he reported too often on the club and its members. As he wrote on Gawker: 'I chose my dignity. Kidding! I mean, I chose trashy gossip.' Unlike Spiers, Sicha did not see the site as a prelude to a print career, and so he did not consider himself an apprentice to his influential subjects. Unlike Peck, he had not written novels, so his 'trashy gossip' could not hurt him in another field. But the cost of this independence was that he had nowhere to turn. His situation had few of the privileges that belong to rec-ognized journalists, protected by an institution and the justification of public events and public subjects.

All Sicha could depend upon was a shifting boundary between people like himself, who were momentarily positioned to observe others, and people who were in positions to be observed. He found his own ways to formulate this unique structure. For instance, there were those who picked up the tab at Soho House, and those who strategically hid in the bathroom.

One year after Sicha became editor, Denton promoted him to the new position of Gawker Media 'editorial director.' At the time, Gawker Media consisted of six sites, and it was rumored that Denton hoped to have at least twelve publications, like Condé Nast publisher S. I. Newhouse. Statistically, Denton's most successful site was the pornography specialist Fleshbot, which he ranked at six million pageviews per month in June 2004. Gawker had two million per month, still an impressive number, but growth had slowed during Sicha's last months as editor. Denton's choice for the next editor was made under real pressure to revamp the flagship site.

Jessica Coen, who replaced Sicha in August 2004, was 24 years old, even younger than Spiers when she had started. Coen had grown up in Los Angeles and returned there after college. As a bored film studio assistant, she kept a blog, where she published widely circulated synopses of *OC* episodes and analysis of celebrity gossip. When Coen announced on her blog that she planned to move to New York, she had just been accepted to Columbia Journalism School: she was going to professionalize. Denton and Sicha, who had read Coen, persuaded her to edit Gawker instead, and the site once again belonged to a young woman newly arrived to the city.

There are several reasons why this must have

seemed like a good idea. One was that Coen, who was young, unpracticed, and ambitious, probably reminded Denton and Sicha of Elizabeth Spiers. Another is that Coen, in fact, had more in common with Sicha. She had grown up close to a public and picked-over media sphere and seemed to be deeply involved in her own resentment and enjoyment of her material. Like Sicha, she took apart people whom she watched carefully but found very distant.

Coen edited Gawker for two years, twice as long as either Spiers or Sicha. From the beginning, she had a more difficult job. Reading Coen's first few months at Gawker, you get the sense of a young woman who works very hard, whose friends think she's funny, and who's been tasked with impersonating an older, much worldlier gay man. Her assignment, it seems clear, was to take the most successful elements of Sicha's model and blow them up. Even Sicha probably couldn't have done it: six months after his promotion, he left to write for the *New York Observer*.

Gawker had always sold itself as mean but it now became, actually, very mean. Sicha, who liked to pretend to be a news organization, had sent 'correspondents' and 'interns' to official media events. Coen found more of them, and she sent them not only to launches and readings but also to private parties, where they took embarrassing party photos. This was the important development: the decision to treat every subject, known or unknown, in public or private situations, with the fascinated ill will that tabloid magazines have for their subjects. Spiers had invented the best-known element of Gawker, 'Gawker Stalker,' which compiled reports of celebrity encounters. Really this had started as a support group for Condé Nast assistants, who wrote in to say what it felt like to see Anna Wintour in person and, also, what she was wearing. As the feature expanded, under Spiers and Sicha, it remained a record of that nice New York moment: seeing a Hollywood face. During Coen's tenure, Gawker Stalker morphed from a list, to a list with photographs, to an interactive map that tracked its subjects through Manhattan with unnerving immediacy.

Coen also retained her sincere interest in tabloids, and soon Gawker was covering the story that actress Tara Reid's shirt had fallen off at P. Diddy's 35th birthday. The site's ratings that month more than doubled. Within a few more months, Coen had posted 'The Fred Durst Sex Tape You Never Wanted.' When their material was less explicit, as it was bound to be when dealing with New York media or literature, the Gawker editors felt compelled to compensate by making up vivid descriptions. So Intern Alexis, reporting on the *New York Times Book Review* redesign, wrote: 'Can we look forward to tales of backroom deals involving Jonathan Franzen and Leisl [*sic*] Schillinger snorting cocaine off of Alice Munro's breast? We hope so!'

If they had only pursued Tara Reid, Fred Durst, and other amateur celebrity pornographers, Gawker simply would have become another version of its own, Denton-owned, Los Angeles spinoff, Defamer.com. Instead, Coen took it upon herself to defame all-but-anonymous people who, within the context of the New York media apparatus, might have seemed like the equivalent of ingénue actresses and other easy-target celebrities.

Taking the form but lacking the content of tabloid magazines and websites, Coen and a succession of guest and co-editors besieged essentially private people, who for the most part did not have the audience or influence of Gawker. Part of this must have been a misunderstanding. Coen had read and written about Nicole Richie, a celebutante who had become known for posing with her father Lionel outside Hollywood clubs. At Gawker, Coen and the other editors delivered the Richie treatment not only to Richie herself but also to Tim Russert's son, who was a student at Boston College and kept a Facebook.com profile, on which he posted a photograph of himself in a hot tub surrounded by girls in bikinis. Gawker ran the photo and summarized Russert's profile by saying that he 'enjoys Golden Tee, Xbox, and someday hopes to share a plate of buffalo wings with a hot bitch.' Perhaps he deserved this; but it seemed incongruous and cruel, to thousands of adults in New York.

This was one type of subject that Gawker chose; another was the subject that had opened itself to criticism but, in fact, did not have much security or influence.

Gawker kept up the heat on the poor alternative week-lies that were being decimated by the advent of free online classifieds. The *New York Press*, Gawker wrote, was 'kind of like a blog, but more expensive for the publisher and less potential for profit. What a smart business model.' Which seemed unfair, because it was true – the *Village Voice* and the *Press*, unlike Gawker, were falling apart. Then, in early 2006, Gawker broke the story that Nick Sylvester, a 23-year-old editor at the *Voice*, had fabricated parts of a cover article. This was a particular kind of scandal: a journalistic ethics viola-tion. But for weeks after it stumbled onto real news, Gawker ran Sylvester through the fictional drama of a Hollywood story. Photos of the reporter ran next to headlines like: 'Putting Nick Sylvester on Suicide Watch.' Months later, it was 'Sylvester Continues Pick-ing Up the Pieces.'

In mid-2006, ratings at Gawker stalled again, and Denton fired Coen's co-editor (the site had become too big, in a way, for just one editor to post content, though one editor remained the star). Coen herself soon left to do online work for *Vanity Fair*. She was replaced by another young woman, Emily Gould, and the cy-cle of education, sarcasm shading into cruelty, against the backdrop of New York and its corruption, began again. The outright nastiness and tabloid-obsession of the late Coen era ended, though the site began to drift a little, in its focus.

Through all the editors and changes at Gawker, one person remained: Nick Denton. His achievement is beyond question: he developed a business that works like a major print publisher. Gawker Media makes its money the same way as Condé Nast – high-end advertisers – and Denton has constructed a similar hierarchy of publishers, editorial directors, managing editors, and so on, to produce his content. The one crucial difference between Gawker Media and its print precursors is that Gawker costs so much less to produce. The costs of online publishing are almost nonexistent, and Gawker editors, whom Denton hires as unknown outsiders, work for the income of well-paid assistants.

Low costs wouldn't mean much, however, if Gawker Media didn't, despite its small budget, attract impressively wealthy and well-connected readers and in turn the appropriate high-paying advertisers. The most remarkable thing Denton has done is eliminate the inefficiency and inflation of the Condé Nast model and then select, as his first target audience, people who work for Condé Nast. The people who produced the mainstream media were, as Denton understood, terminally self-involved and, at least at the top, impossibly overrated. So Gawker analyzed manifestations of their self-indulgence, in their work and private lives, and Denton profited from this. The purpose of Gawker Media was always to improve on the print publishing business model. It was never, as the content of Gawker sometimes seemed to suggest, to produce investigative critiques of the waste that model created. The content at Gawker, like most Condé Nast publications, is a service to the advertisers.

No one ever said Nick Denton was an altruist. But it's important to note that Gawker Media was designed to compete with the corporations that Gawker abused from the sidelines, because this is what created the dissonance of the site's later years. From the beginning, it was crucial that Denton hire novice writers for Gawker, not to mention the rest of his titles. These writers came cheap, and they also were useful in their real fascination with their self-important subjects. It was the writers, from Elizabeth Spiers to Emily Gould, who sold Denton's cynical project to his cynical audience, on the strength of their authentic interest in the material (even when that interest was as conflicted as Choire Sicha's).

But this agreement between Denton and his hires was based on a misunderstanding. The Gawker editors have always been forthright about the fact that what they wanted was to leave Gawker – its low pay and marginal status – and work for the people they maligned. This stance was supposed to give them more credibility; it was also a form of flattery. Furthermore, it was the truth. But in fact they already were working for a media corporation that functioned more effectively but in the same way as the ones they criticized, and as media players the Gawker editors had become more powerful than many of their targets. Gawker retained the stance of a scrappy start-up and an attitude of populist resentment toward celebrities and insiders, even as it became the flagship publication of an online media empire. The status of Gawker rose as the overall status of its subjects declined, and it was this that made Gawker appear at times a reprehensible bully. You could say that as Gawker Media grew, from Gawker's success, Gawker outlived the conditions for its existence.

In early 2007, Choire Sicha – the outsider, the non-careerist, the one who had known restraint, whose parody of journalism had retained some memory of journalism's ethics – returned from the *Observer* to try to save Gawker. But it was too late. The site's default mode was a vacuous sarcasm: that was Gawker. And people liked it: So far this year, the site is averaging ten million page views per month.

Marco Roth

– The Rise of the Neuronovel –

The last dozen years or so have seen the emergence of a new strain within the Anglo-American novel. What has been variously referred to as the novel of consciousness or the psychological or confessional novel – the novel, at any rate, about the workings of a mind – has transformed itself into the neurological novel, wherein the mind becomes the brain. Since 1997, readers have encountered, in rough chronological order, Ian McEwan's *Enduring Love* (de Clérambault's syndrome, complete with an appended case history by a fictional 'presiding psychiatrist' and a useful bibliography), Jonathan Lethem's *Motherless Brooklyn* (Tourette's syndrome), Mark Haddon's *Curious Incident of the Dog in the Night-Time* (autism), Richard Powers's *The Echomaker* (facial agnosia, Capgras syndrome), McEwan again with *Saturday* (Huntington's disease, as diagnosed by the neurosurgeon protagonist), *Atmospheric Disturbances* (Capgras syndrome again) by a medical school graduate, Rivka Galchen, and John Wray's *Lowboy* (paranoid schizophrenia). And these are just a selection of recently published titles in 'literary fiction.' There are also many recent genre novels, mostly thrillers, of amnesia, bipolar disorder, and multiple personality disorder. As young writers in Balzac walk around Paris pitching historical novels with titles like *The Archer of Charles IX*, in imitation of Walter Scott, today an aspiring novelist might seek his subject matter in a neglected corner or along some new frontier of neurology.

What makes so many writers try their hands and brains at the neuronovel? At the most obvious level, the trend follows a cultural (and, in psychology proper, a disciplinary) shift away from environmental and relational theories of personality back to the study of brains themselves, as the source of who we are. This cultural sea change probably began with the exhaustion of 'the linguistic turn' in the humanities, in the 1980s, and with the discredit psychoanalysis suffered, around the same time, from revelations that Freud had discounted some credible claims of sexual abuse among his patients. Those philosophers of mind who had always been opposed to trendy French poststructuralism or old-fashioned Freudianism, and the mutability of personality these implied, put forth strong claims for the persistence of innate ideas and unalterable structures. And in neuroscience such changes as the mind did endure were analyzed in terms of chemistry. By the early '90s, psychoanalysis – whether of a Lacanian and therefore linguistic variety, or a Freudian and drive-oriented kind – was generally considered bankrupt, not to mention far less effective and more expensive than the psychiatric drugs (like Prozac) that began to flow through the general population's blood-stream. The new reductionism of mind to brain, ea-gerly taken up by the press – especially the *New York Times* in its science pages – had two main properties: it explained proximate causes of mental function in terms of neurochemistry, and ultimate causes in terms of evolution and heredity.

Many scientists and philosophers acknowledge that they understand more about how damaged brains work – or, rather, don't work – than about the neuro-chemistry of the normal brain. And yet, in its popu-lar journalistic form, the new reductionism can or will soon describe all human behavior, from warfare to soul-making. The British physician, philosopher, and neuro-skeptic Raymond Tallis has summarized the doctrine: 'A convergence of evolutionary theory, neuroscience, and other biological disciplines has led countless thinkers to claim that we are best understood as organisms whose entire panoply of behavior is di-rectly or indirectly related to organic survival.'

New scientific discoveries may be less important for the change in the novel than the triumphal march of scientific advancement recounted in books like Daniel Dennett's *Consciousness Explained* (1991) and Steven Pinker's *How the Mind Works* (1997). Culture-shaping institutions like the *Times* can't easily respond to Dennett's and Pinker's arguments and analyses, which the average journalist remains unprepared to evaluate, but it has been impossible to ignore their superbly confident rhetoric. Here is the philosopher Dennett:

Fiery gods driving golden chariots across the skies are simple-minded comic-book fare compared to the ravishing strangeness of contemporary cosmology, and the recursive intricacies of the reproductive machinery of DNA make [Bergson's] *élan vital* about as interesting as Superman's dread kryptonite. When we understand consciousness – when there is no more mystery – consciousness will be different, but there will still be beauty, and more room than ever for awe.

The program was to develop a full redescription of consciousness in scientific terms. A corollary program in philosophy of mind was the 'eliminativism' of Paul and Patricia Churchland, who dismiss 'folk psychological' terms (such as happiness, sadness, excitement, anxiety, et cetera) as constituting a hopelessly and indeed meaninglessly imprecise vocabulary without bearing on the actual activities of the brain.

In 1949, Lionel Trilling could write, 'A specter haunts our culture – it is that people will eventually be unable to say, 'They fell in love and married,' let alone understand the language of *Romeo and Juliet*, but will as a matter of course say 'Their libidinal impulses being reciprocal, they activated their individual erotic drives and integrated them within the same frame of reference.' The joke is now quaint; the possibility of an orthodox everyday Freudianism turned out to be no more ultimately threatening than the other specter

Trilling was alluding to. Today people, or a certain class of university-educated ones, are likelier to read books like *The Female Brain* than to consult any psycho-analytic writer on female sexuality, and to send emails like this almost serious one I received from a friend:

In advance of your date in Brooklyn, there are one or two things to know and one or two things to get ready to do! First we should hope that N is post-menstrual and therefore on an estrogen up. Day twelve of the menstrual cycle would be best. Testosterone will be kicking in with a bit of androgen on top of the estrogen, making N somewhat aggressively sexual. Of course she will also be speeding toward ovulation and will be at her verbal and intuitive best. So, use a condom and do a lot of looking in her eyes (girls are prewired at birth for mutual gazing, unlike boys). Give her a lot of face. Her capacity to read emotions and her need to evaluate the facial expressions of those around her will be at a peak (setting in motion circuits established during estrogen flushes in utero and the massive estrogen marination which took place during infantile puberty and hyped-up during adolescence).

So: smile!

In this language, one now needs more words than ever to say 'They fell in love,' and we haven't even got past the first minute of the first date.

This is a problem: what to do after psychoanalysis, and before Dennett's mystery-banishing total explana-tion of consciousness has arrived? Of course it's not as if mid-century novels were case studies written in Freudian jargon. But an era in which analysis, rather than neurology, was taken to offer the most authoritative account of personality was an era more friendly to the informal psychological explorations of novelists. After all, introspection of the self and observation of others were Freud's main tools – as they remain the novelist's.

The change we are discussing here was arrestingly summarized in one of the rare recent novels of psychoanalysis, Daniel Menaker's *The Treatment* (set in the early 1980s but published in 1998). In our new age – or so complains Dr. Morales, the oracular shrink in Menaker's novel – 'Treatment will no longer consist of explorations of significance and spirit and mystery, but quick fixes, twelve steps, behavioral adjustment, and pills.' Morales's elegy for the old ways, delivered in a comic Cuban accent, begins with a claim to be the last Freudian,

the last of a line that stretches from Moses to Aristotle through Cicero to our good Lord Jesus Christ and Aquinas and Maimonides and Shakespeare and Montaigne and finally to Freud and then to me. A line of fascination with and respect for the dignity, the very concept of the human soul. . . . Freud will die, as Marx will die. And all that will be left of those nineteenth century giants of intellect will be the unpityingly neutral doctrines of Sharles Darwin. Darwin is the man who must bear the responsibility for the end of meaning.

Ian McEwan's *Enduring Love* (1997) effectively in-augurates the genre of the neuronovel, and remains one of its more nuanced treatments. The narrator, Joe Rose, is a science journalist, a self-styled man of the enlightenment. Elitist but meritocratic, Joe is given to saying things to his girlfriend like 'Don't you think I'm some kind of evolutionary throw forward?' Despite this weakness for self-congratulation, he is a decent guy who has the bad luck to become the object of a love with no cause but the deluded lover's neurochemistry. The demon lover, one Jed Parry, meets Joe for the first time as part of a group of men trying to save a boy from being blown away in a hot air balloon. The accident, or accidents, happen while Joe is on a picnic with his girlfriend Clarissa, a Keats scholar.

Because he is a science writer by profession, McEwan's Joe is a narrator of realist fiction capable of reflecting on his realism, or rather Zola-esque naturalism. An addict of facts, Joe provides an alibi for McEwan's moments of lyricism – 'The silence appeared so rich as to have a visual quality, a sparkle or hard gloss, and a thickness too, like fresh paint' – and can also comment, in the next sentence, 'This synesthesia must have been due to my disorientation.' Joe correctly diagnoses the madman relatively early in the novel; it's convincing everyone else he's right that takes time. His girlfriend won't believe him and neither will the police until the final scene, when Parry holds a knife to Clarissa's throat. Suffering from de Clérambault's, Parry is beyond reason or persuasion – as Joe (a Darwinian) had always alleged.

In 1997, McEwan was still the sort of writer to challenge somewhat the correctness of Joe's neurological reductionism. Joe's rejection of any talking cure in favor of a thoroughgoing evolutionary psychology and medicalization had costs that the novelist tried to acknowledge: 'From day one,' Clarissa the humanist writes to Joe, 'you saw [Parry] as an opponent and you set about defeating him, and you – we – paid a high price . . . Do you remember me suggesting to you early on – the night you walked out on me in fury – that we ask him in and talk to him? You just stared at me in disbelief, but I'm absolutely certain that at that time Parry didn't know that one day he would want you dead. Together we might have deflected him from the course he took.'

This balanced weighing-up of the case no longer attracts McEwan as a writer. He has now firmly taken sides in a debate he was earlier content to stage with some subtlety. As he confided in a recent *New Yorker* profile, 'Poor Greg [McEwan's son] had to study *Enduring Love* in school. He had a female teacher. And he had to write an essay: Who was the moral center of the book? And I said to Greg, "Well, I think Clarissa's got everything wrong." He got a D. The teacher didn't care what I thought. She thought that Joe was too "male" in his thinking. Well. I mean, I only wrote the damn thing.'

Perhaps so that no one would miss the point again, McEwan largely abandoned his earlier ambiguity when he wrote *Saturday* (2005), in favor of stark biological determinism. That novel evokes recent history – September 11, the street protests against the Iraq war – but only as background music incidental to a central conflict. This is the struggle between mental normals – who are really exceptional normals like the neurosurgeon Perowne, his barrister wife, and their musician son and poet daughter – and the subnormal Baxter, a violent thug suffering from the incurable, genetic brain-wasting disease Huntington's chorea. Here McEwan changes the narrative voice from the first person of *Enduring Love* to a more authoritative limited omniscient third person. We're always in Perowne's scientific mind, a mind capable of reflecting on itself in up-to-date terms of neuroscience, though we also catch glimpses of his creator guiding us, as in the surgeon's reflections on the superiority of neuroscience to ordinary language. When Perowne drives by an antiwar demonstration, a host of half thoughts arise, on war, death, terrorism, the justness of the cause. A voice tells us that all this occurs in 'the pre-verbal language that linguists call mentalese. Hardly a language, more a matrix of shifting patterns, consolidating and compressing meaning in fractions of a second . . . Even with a poet's gift of compression, it could take hundreds of words and many minutes to describe.' Of course McEwan has almost done just that, even down to the color of

Perowne's thoughts – 'a sickly yellow' – but only while conceding the insufficiency of his chosen medium, like a painter ruing the fact that he is not a photographer.

Despite how often we're told that Huntington's disease is the main cause of Baxter's uncontrolled aggression and wild mood swings, it's still tempting to declare him, rather than the neurosurgeon, the most human character in *Saturday*. Blindsided by a car that shouldn't be there, then lied to, and humiliated in front of his friends, he is a wronged man seeking revenge. When he's about to rape Perowne's daughter, he's momentarily bedazzled and soothed by her impromptu poetry recitation and gets knocked into a coma. Ah, the evolutionary advantages of memorizing Mathew Arnold!

By the novel's lights, however, Baxter is simply an incurable. *Saturday* turns into a defense of post-Thatcherite Britain's class system as well as the global imbalance of power by substituting the medical for the social. Some people are simply thugs, for reasons with nothing to do with social organization; in this respect they resemble terrorists. As Perowne reflects, 'There are people around the planet, well-connected and organised, who would like to kill him and his family and friends to make a point.' Perowne knows there is no talking to such people, and this time the novel contains no Clarissa to propose to him that conversation might have spared bloodshed.

In McEwan's work, the neurologically abnormal are foils more than actual characters; their main purpose is to be defeated by normals of the better sort.

But there is another set of neurological novels in which the author inhabits a cognitively anomalous or abnormal person and makes this character's inner life the focus of the novel, soliciting our sympathies. McEwan's neuronovels are of the hard variety; these other books are soft neuronovels.

Books like Lethem's *Motherless Brooklyn* (1999), with its Tourettic narrator, load almost the entire burden of meaning and distinctiveness onto their protagonists' neurologically estranged perceptions of our world. In doing so, they move what has traditionally been a minor character to the front of the novel. Idiots or the insane can dispense ironic wisdom – think of Shakespeare's pretension-puncturing fools – or serve as objects to show off the protagonist's sympathy and understanding in novels like Balzac's *Médecin de Campagne* or Dickens's *Nicholas Nickleby*. Septimus Smith, the schizophrenic or shell-shocked First World War vet in *Mrs. Dalloway*, offers a contrast to the bright world of postwar, aristocratic London, as well as a useful sympathetic object for Woolf's title character. There are also the more existentially troublesome Pip in *Moby Dick* and, of course, American literature's signature idiot, Benjy in Faulkner's *The Sound and the Fury*. And yet it would be strange, if not impossible, to retell the *The Sound and the Fury* exclusively from

Benjy's point of view, which is in effect what many of the neuronovels set out to do.

In *Motherless Brooklyn*, the orphaned narrator afflicted (or blessed) with Tourette's syndrome determines to solve the mystery of his beloved boss's most foul and unnatural murder. This boss was the man who gave him a chance in life, and has been knocked off by his brother. The plot is *Hamlet* by way of Philip Marlowe. The novel shows an agreeable openness about its derivative character, and perhaps the real purpose of such a conceit, poised between high and low, between realism and genre fiction, is to provide cover for the author to engage in the kind of stylistic experimentation habitual to modernist novelists doing interior monologues. Faulkner's Benjy spoke in a strange and addled voice – but then so did Faulkner's other characters, along with those of Joyce, without their needing to be mentally damaged. When Lethem's Tourettic narrator describes himself as 'a human freak show,' 'a carnival barker, an auctioneer, a downtown performance artist, a speaker in tongues, a senator drunk on filibuster,' this justifies or excuses the freewheeling language of his creator. While posing as a sort of observing doctor, like Oliver Sacks, the author indulges an experimental impulse that would today otherwise be seen as pretentious. The modernist desire to gather and combine the heterogeneous voices of entire regions and nations – 'to forge in the smithy of my soul the uncreated conscience of my race' – led to novels open to the whole range of human language, from curses to visionary lyricism. When Lethem puts his words into the mouth of a Tourettic character, the very act of medicalization marginalizes the experimental impulse, marking any remnant modernism as a case for abnormal psychology.

The entire effect of Lethem's neurologically prompted 'carnival barker' is similar to the one contained in the sentences from McEwan quoted above: 'The silence appeared so rich as to have a visual quality, a sparkle or hard gloss, and a thickness too, like fresh paint. This synesthesia must have been due to my disorientation.' The reader is presented simultaneously with an effect and a diagnosis of its cause; the writer indulges in some fancy language or rare perceptions, and then hastens to explain why, on medical grounds, this is allowed.

The *Motherless Brooklyn* model – which is also followed by Haddon's *Curious Incident of the Dog in the Night-Time*, Galchen's *Atmospheric Disturbances*, and Wray's *Lowboy* – in fact attempts a synthesis between what had seemed to be two distinct and increasingly divergent modes: on the one hand, American realism, ending with the 'research novel' – novels stuffed with facts, names, things, impressing the reader with the author's store of 'nonfiction' knowledge – and, on the other hand, the novel of consciousness, of interiority, of linguistic play and estranging description associated with high modernism.

But to ground special perceptions and heightened

language in neurological anomaly ends up severely circumscribing the modernist project. The stylistic novelty and profound interiority of *Ulysses* or *To the Lighthouse* were called forth by normal protagonists – an ad salesman, a housewife – and were proposed as new ways of describing everyone and anyone from the inside out. Modernism seemed revolutionary as long as it threatened to become general; the neuronovel re-fashions modernism as a special case, odd language for describing odd people, different in neurological kind, not just degree, from other human beings. In this way, the 'experimental' writing of neuronovelists actually props up rigid social conventions of language use. If modernism is just the language of crazy, then real men must speak like Lee Child.

Galchen's *Atmospheric Disturbances* exhibits the perils of this mixture of objective (medical) realism with an attempt to write a novel of subjectivity. The novel is narrated entirely from the point of view of Leo Liebenstein, a man who, suffering from Capgras syndrome, believes his wife has been replaced by an exact replica. The delusion sets in when Liebenstein wakes up, Gregor Samsa–like, from uneasy dreams – and a migraine. 'I was then a fifty-one-year-old male psychiatrist with no previous hospitalizations,' he tells the reader, as though giving a medical report on himself. What happens next, however, and for the subsequent 200 or so pages, is not a medical report but the flight of a damaged mind. Liebenstein, who still believes he can tell sane from insane – he's a psychiatrist, after all – decides to go in search of his 'real' wife.

In a gentlemanly review, James Wood placed *Atmospheric Disturbances* in the European modernist tradition of the unreliable narrator, like Hamsun's *Hunger* or Svevo's Zeno's *Conscience*, as well as the novel of love, like Proust's *Un Amour de Swann*. Galchen's novel, he claims, 'is a relentless exploration of how a man could fail to see clearly the woman he loves. We are all afflicted at times with the cataracts of the quotidian, where routine clouds our ability to notice what we once loved about the person we live with – this is the novel's universal appeal.' 'Cataracts of the quotidian' is a lovely phrase, but in order to write it, Wood must blur his own vision. For it is not the case, as Wood suggests, that 'Leo has, perhaps, a version of Capgras syndrome, whose victims come to think that an impostor has replaced a family member or friend.' There is no 'perhaps' about it. Leo does have Capgras syndrome, and the novel depends on its medical precision to be something other than the ravings of a lunatic, and an unsympathetic lunatic at that. Liebenstein is vain and annoying, his narration both leaden and showy: 'She, the woman, the possible dog lover, leaned down to de-shoe.' Here is a man who can't say that his wife takes off her shoes. There must be something wrong with his brain. He's also a man who mistakes the verbose for the descriptive: "Oh,' I said, my palms beginning to sweat as random sensuality carbonated up to my cortex.'

After Leo has followed his allegedly missing wife's trail to Argentina, her native country, he comments on the practice of memorializing the missing of the 1970s Dirty War: 'People naturally perseverate on their personal tragedies, even though such perseveration doesn't really serve anyone, neither the living nor the dead. I mean, there's research on these things. It's simply not a practical use of time to think constantly of the dead.' Such a reflection, at once unfeeling and pretentious (why does he have to say 'perseveration'?), is of a piece with Liebenstein's jerkish personality, which his disorder neither explains nor excuses. Meanwhile, Liebenstein's tics and riffs effectively bury the actual plot of the novel: Rema, Liebenstein's wife, who is there the whole time as her husband raves and treats her like an alien, must keep her cool in order to save her marriage. She even runs after him to Argentina. That she thinks the marriage is worth saving at extraordinary cost is assumed but never addressed. The novel, it turns out, makes most sense not from a neurological standpoint, but under the lens of an old-fashioned Freudian interpretation. For we learn that Rema's father may have been 'disappeared' during the Dirty War, although it's possible he just walked out, and we also know that Rema has married a man who would be roughly her father's age, were he still alive, or around. So Rema seems predestined to love an absent older man, an Oedipal rather than neurological mystery – but not one the novel attempts to illuminate.

Of course you can make Liebenstein's delusion into an allegory of a universal condition, as Wood does, but only at the expense of novelistic and medical specificity both. In some way, perhaps we all suspect our loved ones of being impostors – but if this is so, how can it be that some people have Capgras syndrome and most do not? The difference in degree is a difference in kind. But a neuronovel like Galchen's wants to have it both ways – to combine the pathological and the universal. Even as it relies on something like a readerly *meaning impulse* – we want to be able to generalize or approximate or metaphorize the rare neurological condition into some kind of experience compatible with our own – it also baffles and frustrates the same impulse. Any possibility of the necessary interpretive leap is disavowed by the pathological premise of the novel itself. By turning so aggressively inward, to an almost cellular level, this kind of novel bypasses the self, let alone society, or history, to arrive at neurology: privacy without individuality. And the deep logic of the story is likewise not one of irony or fate or comeuppance, but simple contingency; the etiology of a neurological condition is biological, not moral. And mere biological contingency has a way of repelling meaning.

The aesthetic sensation a reader gets from the neuronovel is not the pleasure of finding the general in the particular, but a frustration born of the defeat of the metaphoric impulse. We want to make the metaphor work, to say, 'Yes, we are all a bit like a paranoid schizophrenic sometimes' or, 'Yes, as Mark Haddon's autistic narrator needs to separate the foods on his plate and not let them touch, to sort colors into good and bad, so am I in my impulse to classify a new genre.' But this would be to indulge the worst tendency of literary criticism, whether of a jargony and sectarian or burbling and humanistic type: to insist on meaning or relevance when there isn't any, or when the works themselves actually foreclose it. Instead the reader has to admit to himself that his brain doesn't work like an autistic person's, a Capgras sufferer's, and that when he loves or works or fears or talks, his ordinary neurons fire or misfire for ordinary rather than extraordinary reasons, whatever these may be.

In other words, the neuronovel in its present form presents the experience of a cognitive defeat. We imagine that science might get there, but it hasn't yet. What's strange is that science, as it moves in the direction of a total redescription of the mind in terms of the brain, may merely be replicating and systematizing the earlier insights of the psychological novel. A recent nonfiction book is called *Proust Was a Neuroscientist*. But insofar as the title's claim is true, Proust was a neuroscientist not by cribbing from contemporary case studies, but by observing himself and others outside of any consulting room. Surely the way for a novelist to be a neuroscientist today is still to anticipate rather than follow the discoveries of brain science. It would be no surprise if a novelist could still describe and mimic traits of cognition that neurology can't yet experimentally confirm.

The question, then, is why novelists have ceded their ground to science. And from the writer's perspective, if not from the reader's, an allegorical interpretation of the neuronovel does seem possible. Is the interest in neurological anomaly not symptomatic of an anxiety about the role of novelists in this new medical-materialist world, which happens also to be a world of giant publishing conglomerates and falling reading rates? Are novelists now, in their own eyes and others', only special cases, without specialized and credentialed knowledge, who may at best dispense accurate if secondhand medical (or historical or sociological) information in the form of an entertaining fictional narrative? And is the impulse to write not an inexplicable compulsion, a category of disorder outside the range of normal? Do writers need special institutions that recognize and treat their mental peculiarities, without granting these any special visionary status? (Such institutions are known as MFA programs.) Perhaps the writer also needs an understanding spouse who will not leave him when he creates her double, or a family that tries to accommodate his strange habits. Most novelists also have grounds for fearing that Ian McEwan, tribune of the healthy brain, will defeat them in the combat over readers and their money. To put all this more simply, the neuronovel tends to become a variety of meta-novel, allegorizing the novelist's fear of his isolation and meaninglessness, and the alleged capacity of science to explain him better than he can explain himself.

By comparison with most 19th-century novels, and even with most 20th-century modernist novels of the 'stream of consciousness' school, the neuronovels have in them very little of society, of different classes, of individuals interacting, of development either alongside or against historical forces and expectations. Iris Murdoch (whose fate it was to become better known, through her husband's memoirs, as an Alzheimer's patient than as a novelist) observed that the 20th-century novel had lost both religion and society. A mid-century novelist who wanted to write about society had first to take pains to reconstruct it, to research something that to George Eliot or Dickens had been more or less spontaneously available. And the 20th-century decline of religion meant a common moral frame of reference couldn't be taken for granted either. So postwar writers as different as Nabokov and Sarraute and Bellow were thrown back on themselves. But at least they retained that subject matter: the personal, the self. It now seems we've gone beyond the loss of society and religion to the loss of the self, an object whose intricacies can only be described by future science. It's not, of course, that morality, society, and selfhood no longer exist, but they are now the property of specialists writing in the idioms of their disciplines. So the new genre of the neuronovel, which looks on the face of it to expand the writ of literature, appears as another sign of the novel's diminishing purview.

Emily Witt

– Miami Party Boom –

VILLA VIZCAYA
Date: July 2005
Venue: Villa Vizcaya
Liquor sponsor: Flor de Caña rum

The Villa Vizcaya is one of those Gatsbyesque single-family mansions that have been converted to event spaces. The new owners installed an industrial kitchen to accommodate catering companies and an HVAC system to dissipate the warmth generated by large groups of people. They removed the permanent furniture so gilt chairs could be trucked in for weddings. Guests still had the run of the extensive gardens, but there was no longer anything particularly Gatsbyesque about the place, just a rental tab of $10,000 for a weekend evening.

The Vizcaya was still a very nice event space. From the parking lot, a jungle of banyans and broad-leafed foliage obscured the house. At night, when picking one's way down a path lit with honeycomb floodlights around the ground, there was a feeling of tropical intrigue, followed by awe when the coral mansion finally emerged from the fronds and the vines, a floodlit beacon in the night. This used to be a Xanadu, a neo-Italianate castle built before Miami was even a city, before Miami Beach was even solid land. Where one person saw a mangrove swamp, the mind behind the Vizcaya saw greatness. Thus the first real estate boom began.

Now another real estate boom was happening, here in Miami, where I had just settled (in the gravitational rather than pioneering sense of the word: for several years I had been sinking in a southerly direction, like the pulp in a glass of orange juice). This was my first party. I don't remember much – not even what the party was intended to celebrate – and I took bad notes. The mosquitoes were formidable. I was plastered in sweat. The night was thick and hot and the concrete steps in back descended into still, inky water. The moon hung over all of it: the bay, the stone barge, the topiaries. Corporations were the sponsors. They hung banner ads promoting Clamato; girls in miniskirt uniforms served free mojitos with Flor de Caña rum. I picked up a free copy of a magazine called *Yachts International*. A real-life yacht was moored to the dock out back, and its passengers were drunk and tan.

I stood with my friend Krishna, watching fireworks explode over Biscayne Bay, over the girls serving rum, over the maze hedge and the moss-covered cherubs and the coral gazebos. We sipped our drinks and scratched our mosquito bites. He gazed at the explosions and said, 'The fireworks were so much better at the condo opening I went to last weekend.'

SPA OPENING
Date: July 2005
Venue: Hotel Victor
Gift Bag: Ylang-Ylang-scented bath cube, thong underwear

I moved to Miami from Arkansas to work at an alt-weekly newspaper. My first order of business, after finding an apartment, was to make friends. I appealed to a girl from work to rescue me from loneliness, and she sent me an email about a spa opening at a new boutique hotel on Ocean Drive, steps away from the mansion where Gianni Versace had met his violent end.

I walked up from my new apartment past the deco and neon, past Lummus Park and the homeless people and mounds of malt liquor bottles beneath the stands of palm trees. It wasn't yet dark – this was an early weeknight party. My coworker checked us in with the tan girl at the door with the clipboard. From then on there would always be tan girls with clipboards. We were led to an elevator past tanks filled with pulsing jellyfish lit a glowing indigo. The elevator went down to the basement area where the spa was, and when the door slid open an impossibly tall drag queen greeted us, dressed only in white towels except for the diamonds that twinkled from her earlobes.

Petrova, a woman with a thick Russian accent, stepped in front of the towel-bedecked drag queen and handed us champagne glasses. She said they contained cucumber martinis, but I think it might have been cucumber and 7Up. 'Welcome,' murmured Petrova. She took us on a tour that was like a ride at Disney World. Curtains were pulled aside: behind one was a naked man on a slab of heated marble. Behind the next was a woman having her breasts gently massaged. 'Ew,' said my coworker. We stayed twenty minutes, then collected our gift bags, which contained thong underwear and an effervescent bath cube. I didn't have a bathtub.

HURRICANE KATRINA
Date: August 2005
Venue: My apartment building, South Beach
Liquor Sponsor: My next-door neighbor Brett
Pharmaceutical Sponsor: Ibid
Food: Frozen pizza
Attire: Sweatpants

Maybe nobody remembers now that Hurricane Katrina hit Miami before New Orleans, but it did, as a baby hurricane. Then it crawled over to the Gulf of Mexico and turned into a monster.

On the afternoon of Katrina I waited too long to wrap my computer in a trash bag and leave work, and the outer bands of the storm were laying into the city by the time I drove across the causeway from downtown to Miami Beach, my car shuddering in the wind. I understood I was to buy nonperishable food items.

The grocery store was chaos, and I was completely soaked from the trip across the parking lot. While I considered the selection of almonds, the power went out. A dramatic hush fell upon us. One minute the store was all beeping scanners and fluorescent lights, the next darkness and total silence but for the wind and rain. I ate some almonds. In the darkness someone broke a wine bottle.

We were told to move to the front of the store. Minutes passed. Rain pounded, wind howled. Suddenly a generator turned on, creating just enough electricity to bathe the store in low-key mood lighting, enough for us to grab bottled water and get out but not enough to forget that the hurricane was something to be taken seriously.

Outside, Biscayne Bay, normally tranquil, was a mountainous expanse of gray and white in extreme motion. Plastic bags flew through the air. The high-rises looked exposed and frail, the dozens of cranes in Miami's skyline like toothpick structures that would come crashing down with the first gust of storm. Once safely home, I put on my pajamas and uncorked a bottle of wine. I opened my door to a blast of wind, rain, and sand that filled my apartment with leaves. I ran across to my neighbor Brett's place, on the other side of the stoop. He opened his door and his apartment filled with leaves.

A friend in Miami once referred to Florida as 'America's funnel,' and that's what I'd thought of when

I met Brett. He was in his mid-30s and had dyed black hair, stained teeth, and a permanent sunburn, and was almost always smoking on our building's stoop and drinking from a bottle of Tequila Sauza. His apartment was draped in fabric of different psychedelic patterns. He had been looking forward to Burning Man. He had played in an early-'90s grunge rock band of some re-pute – they had toured with the Smashing Pumpkins – but things hadn't worked out very well. In a moment of idle gossip one afternoon, my landlord Dave told me that Brett had woken up one morning after a night of substance abuse in New York and found his girlfriend dead next to him. So he took their cat and moved to Miami, and now the cat was in its waning days and Brett was selling boats on the internet, supposedly.

Once I left him my rent check to give to Dave, since I was at the office most days. The next morning Dave, a tan surfer type from Boca Raton who never seemed upset about anything, knocked on my door. 'Um,' he said, embarrassed. 'Don't give your rent check to Brett.'

But Brett was the social nexus of our building, which was a low-rent holdout in a neighborhood at the bottom tip of South Beach that had gotten much, much fancier since Brett moved in. Our building was funny – the walls of most of the apartments had vari-ously themed murals: underwater scenes, jungle scenes, and, my favorite, in the studio behind mine, hot-air balloons and clouds. My guess is that the landlords originally painted the murals as a sort of spell against the crack-addicted undead that were said to have ruled the neighborhood in the early '90s. The building even used to have some kind of tiki setup on the roof, but the door to the roof was padlocked when the rule of law finally arrived, sometime around the turn of the century. My apartment was painted the colors of a beach ball and included sloping wood floors, bamboo shades, and a mosaic tile counter. It was a one-room studio and a total dump, but it had beach style.

Our two-story baby-blue building was surrounded by towering new condominiums of gleaming white stucco, one of which had a helicopter landing pad. I saw a helicopter land exactly once in the two years I lived there. Rent was month-to-month, which meant I was the only person in the building with a salary.

Upstairs lived a call girl with whom Brett was good friends. She would come down sometimes in her evening finery and ask Brett if he would 'do her,' meaning would he please fasten her black lace bustier to maximize the lift of her fake breasts. Brett would flash his tobacco-stained teeth, hook her into her corset, pat her bum, and reassure her that he would do her anytime. They were fond of each other.

She didn't like me, with good reason. She lived above me, in a jungle-themed studio. Once, when I was sitting on my couch on a Saturday morning, a thin stream of amber-colored liquid began to patter steadily on my windowsill from somewhere upstairs. Fuck this,

I thought. I went upstairs and banged on her door, asking why somebody was peeing out the window. It was that kind of building. She said that she had spilled a cup of tea. 'Peeing out the window!' she yelled. 'What kind of trash do you think I am?' I apologized, but the damage was done. Later she moved back home to Michigan, leaving in a sweatshirt, with no makeup on. But that was much later, when everyone was leaving.

Brett's friends were always hanging around, none of them model citizens, but I would regularly cross our foyer to chat with them, because being alone at the end of the day sometimes felt unbearable. Two months in, my friend-making campaign was going only so-so.

The night Hurricane Katrina hit Miami, Brett had a pizza defrosting in the oven – the power wasn't yet knocked out – and he dispensed Tombstone, Percocet, and beer. This combo hit me quickly, and I soon staggered home. It was raining so hard that a puddle had seeped under my door. As the streetlights flickered and the eye of the storm passed over the city, I slept.

I woke up the next morning and drove to work. I assumed that the rest of the city still had electricity, but it turned out that almost nobody did – some wouldn't get it back for two weeks. Downtown Miami was deserted. The stoplights were out. The only movement was that of a tribe of vagrants deeply concerned with the transportation of fallen palm fronds scattered across sidewalks and intersections. I arrived at the New Times building. Its parking lot was empty except for palm fronds. I sat there for a full minute, engine idling, before turning around and driving back down the Biscayne Corridor. Even the windows of the Latin American Café were darkened, the spy shop shuttered, the sidewalks damp and empty but for the Sisyphean struggle of man versus palm frond. You wouldn't think electricity makes that much of a difference during the day, but it makes a world of difference.

THE MTV VIDEO MUSIC AWARDS
Date: August 2005
Venues: Pawn shop lounge, the Redroom at Shore Club, backseat of a police car, La Carreta 24-hour takeout window, Hibiscus Island, someone's yacht
Liquor sponsors: Various
Food: Empanadas, roast suckling pig, cigarettes
Attire: Cowboy boots
Celebrities: Kanye West, Carmen Electra, Jessica Simpson, Black Eyed Peas
Gift bag: One Slim Jim, one Slim Jim T-shirt

Brett was closing on a big internet boat deal 'with some Mexicans' the weekend of the MTV Video Music Awards, and the one party I'd been invited to was canceled because of storm damage. The publicity build-up for the awards had been extensive. I kept seeing press releases on the fax machine at work that said things like HOTEL VICTOR LANDS A SPACE IN THIS

YEAR'S MOST COVETED GIFT BAG. P. Diddy had flown in to a local marina wearing a rocket pack and a white linen suit to announce the nominees. I couldn't go outside without returning with souvenirs like a free Trick Daddy Frisbee handed to me from the trunk of a Louis Vuitton–upholstered muscle car. But my lack of party invitations made me feel sorry for myself. When an event happens in Miami and you have no parties to attend you start to doubt your own self-worth, even if you're a pale myopic person with the salary of a rookie civil servant who has no business at any Miami party, let alone the fancy ones.

Then a friend called from Los Angeles to see if I would go out with his friend, who was in town for the awards. This friend was a Jewish rapper in a hip-hop group called Blood of Abraham, who also co-owned something called a 'lifestyle store' in Miami's Design District. The Design District, much like the Wynwood Arts District, was more of a semiotic hypothesis than a reality. Most people still knew it as Little Haiti, and in spite of skyrocketing housing prices it was one of the poorest urban zip codes in America. Average T-shirt price at the store, which closed down within the year: $70.

This friend of a friend, whose emcee name was Mazik, picked me up with a cousin or two in a shiny white Land Rover. He was wearing a pink polka-dotted shirt and a green sweater vest. He announced that Kanye West was performing downtown and that we were going to see him. I was wearing cowboy boots and a dress I'd bought at a Savers in Little Rock, but somehow Mazik and the cousins and I managed to talk our way into a pawn shop-cum-nightclub through leggy models in stilettos. Kanye West showed up for five minutes and then Carmen Electra performed a choreographed dance with four anemic-looking girls in spangled costumes. The free drinks tasted like lemon drops and when we left we were presented with a gift bag containing a Slim Jim and a Slim Jim T-shirt.

We continued on to the beach, to a hotel called Shore Club. Mazik again was on the list. Outside, under a cluster of Moroccan lanterns, I saw Jessica Simpson sitting on a bench looking lonely. She was very small – midget-size, almost, tan and tiny. In the VIP room I saw a member of the Black Eyed Peas get into a fight. My new friends got peripherally involved, in a drunken inept way, but at least they didn't take off their shirts. Somebody else did, at which point Jessica Simpson was whisked away by what looked like a bodyguard detail dressed up as county sheriffs. We left. The following night, Suge Knight would be shot in the kneecap in that very spot.

Miami is connected to the island of Miami Beach by a series of causeways. The General Douglas E. MacArthur Causeway, I-395, is the main artery into South Beach, the palm tree–lined promenade that Crockett and Tubbs were always driving down on Miami Vice. I drove back and forth across the causeway almost every day of my time in Miami, and it never lost its air of serenity. Because of Florida's flatness, the sky is bigger there; the clouds pile into endless stacks of white Persian cats and mohair bunnies. The MacArthur is bordered on one side by the port of Miami, where massive cruise ships and freighters come and go. When I was heading toward the beach, the view was of glittering white condominiums and yachts. When I was heading toward the city, it was of downtown: luminous skyscrapers growing up from a rickety forest of cranes, half-finished high-rises, and canvas-draped rebar skeletons.

At night sometimes the moon would rise large and yellow over the water and packs of scarablike motorcyclists on Yamahas would whir around my car, occasionally doing wheelies. Even when traffic was bad, the environment was glossy: the shiny surfaces of moonlight on the water, of streetlights on freshly waxed cars; the palm fronds rustling and the revving of German motors and the glow of LCD screens through tinted windows showing pornography.

At the end of the night, inside the marshmallow-white Land Rover, I clutched my Slim Jim gift bag. A row of blue lights flashed behind us. We pulled over and a group of police cars somehow screeched into formation around us, cutting us off in front, reducing traffic on the causeway to a single lane and leaving our car with two-thirds of the highway and a very wide berth on all sides. I'd lost count of how many lemon-drop cocktails I'd had, but I was drunk. We were all drunk. I can say fairly confidently that the driver was drunk, and that all the other drivers on the causeway were drunk too. It was 4:30 on a Saturday morning, and now we were going to be arrested.

The police had their weapons drawn, and emerged from their cars shielded by bulletproof car doors. They yelled into a loudspeaker and we followed their instructions. I stepped out of the car and held my hands in the air. I walked backward, a breeze rippling the palm fronds and my dress, my eyes on the asphalt where normally cars speeded and now all was quiet. I knelt, gazing up at the soft, purple sky. Then I was cuffed and put into the back of a police car next to an empty pizza box, where a lady cop began demanding information about our firearms.

I was suddenly a lot more impressed with the people I'd been hanging out with. They had weapons? I quickly confessed that there had, in fact, been a fistfight. But then it emerged that no, the police had simply confused our car with another white Land Rover. Someone in that Land Rover had fired shots at a police officer. We were sheepishly released, our drunkenness apparently not enough to merit attention from the law. We drove to Little Havana and ate empanadas.

There was one more party that weekend, on Hibiscus Island. We were transported by boat, and the theme was sort of luau-meets-Vegas: tiki torches, roasted suckling pig, and girls in uniform carrying around piles of loose cigarettes on silver platters. I think American Spirit sponsored the party, but maybe it was

Lucky Strike. We removed our shoes and climbed onto a yacht moored against the mansion's back dock. Out in the Gulf, Katrina was growing and New Orleanians were preparing to flee, but the Atlantic was quiet now. It was pretty, with the lights and the palm trees and the views of South Beach, and a little rain that would fall for a minute and stop.

DRIVING BRETT AND ANDY TO THE AIRPORT
Date: September 2005
Venue: Toyota Corolla
Pharmaceutical sponsor: Brett
Gift bag: A very small Ziploc

Brett and a friend of his, an Australian male model named Andy, were going to Burning Man. I agreed to drive them to the airport. Their flight left early, and when I knocked on his door Brett emerged baggy-eyed and smelling like a mildewed sponge soaked in tequila. We picked up Andy at his girlfriend's. She was also a model, tawny with dark brown eyes and a minimalist figure. As they said goodbye they were orbited by what seemed like a dozen teacup Chihuahuas but might only have been two very light-footed teacup Chihuahuas.

We merged onto the highway. Brett, in the back-seat, began emptying his pockets, pulling out bags of pills and empty mini Ziplocs coated in a residue of white dust.

'Should I put those pills in a container?' asked Andy. 'I guess. I don't know. You think?' 'I guess.' Brett passed a baggie of prescription pills to the front seat and Andy put it into an orange case with a prescription on it. 'But what about the cocaine?' 'The cocaine?' 'The cocaine?' I shouted.

'Somebody gave me all this coke last night. I can't bring it?' 'Don't bring it on the airplane.' 'Really?' They decided there was only one thing to do with the cocaine.

As I nervously pulled up to the airport, Brett put what remained in the well next to the gearshift. He looked at his nostrils in the rearview mirror and took a Percocet. I quickly put the baggie in the glove compartment. Off to Burning Man! We waved to each other. I drove to work feeling lonely.

HURRICANE WILMA
Date: October 2005
Venue: Ted's Hideaway, South Beach

Wilma hit Miami in the middle of the night, and by the time I woke in the morning the city was silent, void of electricity. The air felt a way that it would never feel again in Miami: crisp, dry, and cool like a New England fall day. I walked to the beach. Men with surfboards ran past me to catch the only surfable waves there would ever be on South Beach. The wind was still blowing and pelicans loitered miserably, too worn out to flap their wings even when the surfers barreled toward them. Somebody spoke up for the pelicans, and ordered everyone to leave them alone while they were tame like this, docile with exhaustion.

People wandered the streets with cameras, taking photos of smashed cars under fallen trees. One parking lot between two buildings had formed a wind tunnel. The cars had piled up like leaves. This was a popular spot with the photographers. My trunk, which had been stuck shut since a British woman in a gleaming chrome SUV rear-ended me, was suddenly open and filled with the branches of a nearby ginkgo tree.

A curfew was called for nightfall and the city forbade driving after dark. My neighborhood bar was crowded and candlelit, but outside the strange autumnal chill remained. My neighbors picked their way through the darkness, stepping over fallen trees. They held flashlights and lanterns and the landscape seemed odd, like they were going to a Halloween party in Sleepy Hollow. The stars were bright over the darkened city.

Some parts of the city were without electricity for weeks, but my place regained power after three days. Miami Beach with its tourists is always a priority. For the remainder of the time I lived in Florida, skyscrapers had plywood over the places where windows had broken. In poorer neighborhoods blue tarps covered damaged roofs for years. But the significance of Wilma didn't register at the time. Now people say that was the moment when the manna curdled in Miami, when the fragility of its physical location started to affect property values, when the logic of building taller and taller high-rises in a natural-disaster-prone peninsula started to seem suspect. Wilma wasn't even a real storm, it wasn't an Andrew or a Katrina-in-New Orleans, but it was enough.

ART BASEL MIAMI BEACH
Date: December 2005
Venue: Miami Beach Convention Center, my apartment
Celebrities: Jeffrey Deitch, David Lachapelle (rumored),
Madonna (rumored), Sofia Coppola (rumored)

Art Basel Miami Beach is perhaps the only time each year when New York aesthetes bother with Miami. The art fair is an offshoot of Art Basel in Switzerland, and it attracts a lot of very wealthy people. These were a different sort of wealthy people from the banana-yellow-Hummer-driving, highly leveraged 'rich people' who were always cutting each other off on I-95. Suddenly my neighborhood hamlet of fake tans, silicone breasts, and hair gel was invaded by pale androgynous people with Italian glasses. The first rule of fashion in Miami was that you wear nothing that might make you look androgynous or poor. These people all looked like shit, but wonderfully so, expensively so.

I spoke with my friends on staff at various hotels,

who told me that Sofia Coppola had been spotted at the Delano, and that Madonna was at the Visionaire party last night, and that David LaChapelle's poolside installation at the Setai had a live transsexual made of silicone lounging naked in a glass house in the middle of a swimming pool.

NEW YEAR'S EVE
Date: January 2006
Venue: The Delano Hotel
Food: Surf and turf
Liquor sponsor: Dom Perignon
Celebrities: Billy Joel, Snoop Dogg, Jamie Foxx, Ludacris

I ended up at Jamie Foxx's album release party on New Year's Eve because I accepted an invitation from a man twenty years older than me who was the local correspondent for a prominent celebrity tabloid. 'You're the only person I know who is superficial enough to actually enjoy this,' he said, kindly.

I decided I would enjoy myself. The problem was that as soon as I stepped into the lobby of the Delano, with its gossamer curtains and high ceilings, and as soon as I was served champagne by models dressed in silver angel outfits, and primal hunter-gatherer food (fire-blackened meat, stone crab claws, oysters, caviar, lobster tails) by a waiter dressed in tennis whites, I was overwhelmed by a profound sadness.

But 2006 was going to be a good year, or so promised Jamie Foxx when his press handler escorted him over to us. He was covered in distracting surfaces – mirrored sunglasses, diamond earrings, polka-dotted shirt – and graciously shook our hands.

'An excellent year,' he promised, and I believed him.

Then he performed the song 'Gold Digger' against a backdrop of more gossamer curtains and dancing angels and pewter candelabras, while we watched from the lawn around the pool, where the grass was cut short like a tennis lawn and tiny white edelweisslike flowers sprouted. I held my glass of Dom and my high heels sank into the soil. Snoop performed, looking shy and grinning goofily, then Ludacris, and then fireworks exploded over the Atlantic Ocean and a new year began.

I ended the night without my escort, at a bar called Club Deuce. In Florida, unlike in Brooklyn, the dives are really dives: neon lights shaped like naked ladies, wrinkly alcoholics, obese bartenders, all in New Year's crowns, blowing horns and throwing confetti. I was in a cab heading home alone by 4 am, my gold shoes somehow full of sand.

MY 25TH BIRTHDAY
Date: April 2006
Venue: Stand of palm trees, Key Biscayne beach
Liquor sponsor: byob

I celebrated this birthday with my friend Krishna, who made close to six figures a year as a waiter at the most expensive hotel in South Beach. Krishna had grown up in a yoga ashram in Central Florida and then gone to Brown. The son of his ashram's guru was now a big-time real estate broker in Miami Beach with a boat and a BMW and an apartment in the Mondrian. Krishna was gay and surrounded himself with down-to-earth, interesting people. He was a real friend, not a fake friend. Things were changing for me. For example, I started taking tennis lessons. I started hanging out with people I actually liked. I stopped shooting the shit with Brett. I would nod on my way out the door, when he was sitting there having a cigarette, but I didn't go swimming with all his friends in the evenings, and their parties got so depressing. One night, I agreed to drive one of them to 'pick something up.' I was just trying to be neighborly. On the way, the guy failed to warn me about a helpless animal crossing the road. I know that as the driver it was technically my fault, but he saw this animal, this doomed raccoon, and he just let out a slow 'Whoa.' Then I ran over the raccoon. In the rearview mirror I watched the raccoon drag itself toward the curb. I hadn't even properly killed it. I was furious. I was furious at this poor creature for trying to live on Miami Beach, at myself for having maimed it, and especially at this guy for being too much of a stoner to stop me. It wasn't quite fair, but that's how I felt. From then on, when Brett's drug-dealer friends offered cocaine when I stepped out of my apartment in the morning I would be outright rude. At some point Brett had lost his job selling boats.

My relationship with Miami changed. I went to fewer parties at hotels. The gift-bag influx slowed. I stopped being around so many people who sold real estate, who picked me up in luxury vehicles, who drank lychee martinis and said things like, 'Well, I was talking about this with John Stamos at Mansion the other night.' I still pursued unlikely friendships out of curiosity – I went on a date with a paparazzo who had netted his fortune from a single portrait of Paris Hilton with her tiny dog. The funny thing was that this paparazzo had a tiny dog of his own that would nuzzle and burrow under your arm when you held it, like a little cat.

I stopped writing emails to my friends in New York about my mirth at outrageous Floridian real estate nonsense. The billboard advertising a condominium project on I-95 that was simply a photo of a man's hands unhooking a woman's bra was no longer delightfully symbolic of everything that was wrong with the real estate boom, just depressingly so.

To live in a place like Florida is to destroy the earth. I watched snowy egrets and great blue herons picking their way through drainage ditches outside of Costco. I covered county commission meetings where the merits of building suburbs in the Everglades were proclaimed and posters of digitally rendered high-rises were offered in exchange for slackening of the zoning laws. I went to the Everglades and saw anhingas flitting under the boardwalk, their tails expanding like fans in water stained brown like tea. I thought about how in Florida, a bird like the anhinga was only useful insofar as it provided local color in the names of housing developments. The names of new housing developments grew more and more offensive. I started keeping a list. The idea was to make some sort of game out of it, like that internet game that generated Wu-Tang names. I thought I could make a Florida subdivision name generator.

Here is an excerpt of my list: Villa Encantada. Gables Estates. Old Cutler Bay. Journey's End. Hancock Oaks. Cutler Oaks. Pine Bay. Deering Bay Estates. Old Cutler Glen. Cocoplum. Saga Bay, Serena Lakes, Lakes by the Bay, Three Lakes, Cutler Estates. Swan Lake. Arabesque. Arboretum Estates. The Sanctuary at Pinecrest. Gables by the Sea. Tahiti Beach Island. Snapper Creek Lakes. Banyans by the Gables. Coco Ibiza Villas. Kumquat Village. The Imperial. The Moorings. Trocadero in the Grove. Gladewinds. Killian Oaks Estates. The Palms at Kendall. Poinciana at Sunset. Villas of Briar Bay. Las Brisas at Doral. The Courts at Doral Isles. Porto Vita. The Terraces at Turnberry. Lychee Nut Grove. Flamingo Garden Estates. L'Hermitage. The Palace.

NIGHTLY BARBECUE, GUANTÁNAMO BAY
Date: May 2006
Venue: Leeward dormitories, Guantánamo Bay Naval Base
Liquor sponsor: Navy PX

A senior reporter at the paper quit, and they sent me in her stead to report on the detention facilities at Guantánamo Bay. Cuba fell under our purview as a Miami newspaper, even if Gitmo was 400 miles away. Before I left, I watched *A Few Good Men*, the basic-cable mainstay about a military cover-up at Guantánamo. When Demi Moore and Tom Cruise visit the island to look for evidence, Demi, in curve-hugging Navy whites, accuses a flippant Tom of goofing around. 'Are you going to do any investigating,' she demands, 'or did you just come here for the tour?' I came for the tour.

I flew Air Sunshine. A lawyer, a frequent flyer on Air Sunshine propeller planes, had told me that taking the airline's shuttles from Fort Lauderdale to Guantánamo Bay was like traveling in a 'minivan with wings.' The nine-seater's decor was peeling blue pleather accentuated with protruding bits of orange foam. A front-row seat afforded a detailed view of the cockpit, since one sat practically inside of it. The windows were pockmarked and scratched. The engine thrummed a steady bass vibrato. The air smelled acrid with fumes. As the plane tilted to land, a container of shoe polish rolled across the floor.

I spent ten days at Guantánamo, most of it by myself
on the deserted leeward side, where I rented a bicycle
from a Jamaican contract worker and went swimming
on a rocky beach overseen by Marine guard towers.
The detention facilities were on the windward side,
where we could go only with military escorts. I toured
the camps twice, going through the motions of journalism. The tour was a farce. We saw the prisoners only
from a distance. The cells they showed us were stocked
with 'comfort items' like soap, the 'interrogation room'
furnished with a plush armchair and an espresso machine. The troops we spoke with told us about their
scuba-diving lessons. They lived in a suburb devoid of
a city, like an amputated limb with a life of its own,
with Pizza Hut and Ben & Jerry's and outdoor screen-
ings of *The Hills Have Eyes 2*. When inside the camp,
the military personnel removed the Velcro name tags
attached to their uniforms and emphasized that detain-
ees have been known to make threats. On one of the
tours our guide was Naval Commander Catie Hanft,
deputy commander of the Joint Detention Group.
Commander Hanft's previous job was commanding
the Naval Brig in Charleston, South Carolina, where
José Padilla was jailed in an environment of almost total sensory deprivation, never allowed to see the face
of his captors, until his transfer to a federal prison in
Miami. Hanft had short hair and a tan. When one of
our escorts accidentally called her by name she smiled
and interrupted: 'Colonel, don't say my name in the

camp, please.' The mood curdled slightly.

Most nights we would pick up some meat and alcohol at the Navy PX before they escorted us back to the deserted side of the bay. Then we would drink alcohol and grill meat, 'we' being an assortment of human rights lawyers, Pashto translators, and journalists. Joshua Colangelo-Bryan, one of the lawyers, told of walking in on his Bahraini client, Juma Al Dosari, as he attempted suicide during a bathroom break the previous year. Dosari, who had made twelve serious attempts, had cut one wrist and tried to hang himself. On this visit, although Colangelo-Bryan noted a couple of new scars, Dosari seemed in better spirits.

On the night before I left, there was a bigger group than usual at the barbecue. Around midnight, when everyone was slightly drunk, a plane came in to land on the base's runway, which was also on the deserted side of the bay. Sleek and floodlit against the night sky, the plane gleamed white and bore the green insignia of the Saudi royal family on its tail. The Saudis had come for some of the prisoners. In the morning the plane was gone.

NBA FINALS
Date: June 2006
Venue: Street in Coconut Grove

The Miami Heat had had a good season, and as the

team advanced to the playoffs people actually started going to Miami Heat games. Everybody in the stands wore white to these games. Later I was informed that the entire sports blogosphere made fun of Miami for doing that. The Heat beat the Mavericks in the finals. I went to an outdoor screening of the last game and watched Dirk Nowitzki run backward chewing his mouth guard with an increasingly frantic air of frustration. Lots of Miami players seemed to be wearing special injury-preventing compression kneesocks and sleeves. After the team won, a friend who was visiting observed the cheering hordes in white on the street. 'The most hard-core Miami Heat fan is like one of those girls who wears a pink Red Sox shirt,' he said.

FIDEL PUTS RAUL IN CHARGE
Date: August 2006
Venue: Calle Ocho

Everybody wanted to be in Miami when Castro fell. The *Miami Herald* supposedly had a plan, or rather the plan, for the moment of Castro's death. Then nothing turned out as planned. Castro showed up on television in an Adidas tracksuit, looking ill. Then he made his brother president. The streets outside Café Versailles were full of people honking horns and waving flags, but Fidel wasn't really dead. Fidel Castro was no longer president of Cuba, he was attached to a colostomy bag and being fed through a tube, but the Berlin Wall moment everyone in Miami expected didn't happen. For the first time, it seemed possible that it might not ever happen. Then again, he's not dead yet.

DINNER WITH A PSYCHIC
Date: September 2006
Venue: The home of Univision's morning show's visiting psychic

I was writing about the first homosexual love triangle in an American-made Spanish-language telenovela. One of the actors, who was straight (it was unclear whether the show's tolerance extended into telenovela casting practices), invited me to dinner at the house of a Spanish-language television psychic named Frances. I had a friend of a friend in town so I invited him, too, thinking he would enjoy the cultural experience. He did not enjoy it. The evening ended with Frances waving a wand around a warbling vibratory instrument called a meditation bowl and ordering the friend of a friend to hug a palm tree. 'I'm an atheist,' he kept repeating, his face pressed against the palm tree. The next week I got an email inviting me to a gathering at Frances's with some Tibetan monks. I have many regrets, but few loom so large as my decision not to attend.

WEEKNIGHT SHINDIG AT BRETT'S
Date: September 2006
Venue: Our apartment building

This year Brett came back from Burning Man with an announcement: he had fallen in love. Kellie, an 18-year-old from Truckee, California, arrived shortly thereafter. She immediately found work as a cocktail waitress and started supporting him. I gave her my old driver's license so she could get into bars. We had other news as well: our building was going condo.

ART BASEL MIAMI BEACH
Date: December 2006
Venue: Shore Club

This year I went out a little more at Art Basel. I went to a *Vanity Fair* party. We got rubber bracelets, like Lance Armstrong testicular cancer bracelets, but hot pink and stamped VANITY FAIR. My aunt, who lives in southwest Florida and paints pictures of children on beaches flying kites, came to see the art, but what excited her most was watching someone write a $400,000 check in a particleboard boothlet.

A CELEBRATION OF THE JADE COLLECTION OF THI-NGA, VIETNAMESE PRINCESS-IN-EXILE
Date: February 2007
Venue: The Setai, Collins Avenue

The paper assigned me an investigative piece: discover the true identity of Princess Thi-Nga, a Miami Beach philanthropist and supposed member of the exiled imperial family of Vietnam. She was on the board of the Bass Museum of Art, where the parties were always sponsored by Absolut Vodka. Her collection of ancient jade sculpture was on display at the Bass at the time, which some people saw as a conflict of interest. My editor thought she might be a fraud. I failed to uncover much evidence of this. I failed to uncover much evidence at all, actually. It appeared nobody was paying close attention to the lineage of the former royal family of Vietnam. I too didn't really care.

I met Thi-Nga at the Setai, the hotel where my friend Krishna worked. A room at the Setai cost upward of $1,000 a night. Its bar was inlaid with mother-of-pearl and its couches upholstered with manta ray skins, or something like that. According to Krishna, when a guest of the Setai arrived at Miami International Airport, he or she had the choice of being chauffeured in a Bentley or a Hummer (a question of personal style). In the car was a wide selection of bottled-water brands and an iPod.

Thi-Nga was launching her jade sculpture exhibition with an elaborate party at the hotel. I met her there for breakfast the day before the party. I ate a $12 bowl of muesli. It was the most delicious bowl of muesli I have ever eaten.

For her party, Thi-Nga had rented an elephant named Judy. Adorned with gemstones, Judy led a parade down Collins Avenue on Miami Beach that also included dancers: Thai ones with pointy golden hats and splayed fingers and a Chinese lion that batted its paper eyelashes to the rhythm of cymbals. The princess rode in a silver Jaguar convertible behind them, seated next to the mayor of Miami Beach, waving to confused pedestrians who tentatively waved back. Then all her guests went to the Setai and ate salmon.

BRETT MOVES OUT
Date: April 2007

This party is in fact only theoretical. My neighborly relationship with Brett had deteriorated to the point of mere formality, so I'm not sure if he had a goodbye party or not. I hope he had a big party, where the lava lamps oozed and the cigarette butts accumulated and the dollar bills were dusted in cocaine. Our building was depopulated now. The call girl was gone; the dumb stoner who had been my accomplice in the murder of the raccoon was gone. The apartments upstairs had sold for phenomenal amounts of money. My apartment had been purchased by a tennis pro, who informed me that I could consider him a landlord upgrade. I took him at his word and purchased the air-conditioning unit with the highest Consumer Reports rating, paid the alcoholic handyman who hung around the neighborhood to install it, and deducted the whole production from my rent check. Going condo was amazing.

Unless you were Brett. Things weren't going well for Brett, who was still unemployed and being supported by his teenage girlfriend. He and Kellie had recently been arrested for driving someone else's car that happened to have a felony-size quantity of crystal meth in the glove compartment. I encountered them on our stoop after they had been released on bail. Apparently everything would be all right; they had agreed to rat on some drug dealer. But still, this on top of moving. They were heading up to 8th Street, a part of South Beach that remarkably had retained its seedy character, and whose apartments, though as expensive as everything else in Miami, were terrible to live in. I'd had a friend who lived on Brett's new block; her floor was often inexplicably littered with millipede exoskeletons. She would gamely sweep up the hard brown shells and claim that they were harmless, but I vowed that I would draw the line of shitty-apartment-living at mysterious worm infestations.

Then one day Brett was gone, and the landlords were happily ripping out the interior of his apartment.

One of them, Dave, told me it had been a relief.

'You should have seen the bathroom. Drug addicts. It's disgusting.'

Very stupidly, I had never thought of Brett as an addict, just as a guy who did drugs. A certain kind of Miami guy who liked to party. But now Brett was gone. All traces of him were replaced, in a matter of weeks, with granite countertops and track lighting.

I saw him one more time that summer, on 5th Street, when I knew I would be leaving Miami. I was walking home from the gym when I was waylaid by a torrential downpour, the kind where I could see the violent wall of water approaching from across the street. I waited under an overhang, staring at nothing, until it retreated. In the dripping aftermath, the sidewalks gray and clean, the palm trees still quivering, I encountered Brett on a street corner. Brett wasn't a pessimist. Everything was going great, he said, the new apartment was fantastic. Later, when the recession came, I took comfort in knowing that, like me, Brett was probably all right, because Brett owned nothing.

That was the thing about boom times that later became clear: We now know that boom times don't feel like boom times. They feel like normal times, and then they end. Particularly if one is not a direct beneficiary of the excess wealth and one's salary is measly to non-existent, boom times are just the spectacle of other people's reckless spending. Their gluttony was my gluttony of course – only a bore would have abstained from the festivities – but their downfall was little more than an abstraction from the vantage point of one with no assets.

Our downfalls would not involve grand narratives of repossession or foreclosure, just a steadily diminishing ability to keep some fundamental part of the city at bay. In heady days, we conquered Miami, carving out the mangroves, digging up the ocean bottom and slathering it on a sandbar, molding concrete into skyscrapers, pumping refrigerated air through miles of metal windpipes and over glass coffee tables and white couches. But here, now, as those with no assets fled to low-rent holdouts, inland from the beach to paved-over swamps, recession only meant a slow infiltration: worms burrowing through the floor and dying, spores drifting through vents, and terracotta roof tiles uplifted by the autumn winds.

MY LAST DAY
Date: August 2007

The Corolla was packed up, and as I was about to leave, one of those terrific summer rainstorms hit. I lay next to my boyfriend on his bed (for by then I had a boyfriend), watching the rain pound against the windows, the palms lean into the wind, and the cat purr between us. Of the whole tableau, the only thing I anticipated missing was the cat. The relationship was ending, my job was ending, and the real estate boom had already ended. I had gotten ornery in the last months in Miami. If another interviewee told me, as we drove in his golf cart through a maze of pink stucco on top of a leveled mangrove grotto, that he 'lived in paradise,' I thought I might wrestle the wheel from him and plunge us both into the algae blooms of a fertilizer-polluted drainage canal. So I left the place where baby sea turtles mistake the floodlights of condos for the rising sun, where the dogs are small, the breasts are big, and the parties are ornamented with drag queens in bubble baths.

When the rain stopped I drove past suburbs until I hit the Everglades, then emerged into suburbs again on the other side.

Chad Harbach

– MFA vs. NYC –

I n his 2009 book, *The Program Era: Postwar Fiction and the Rise of Creative Writing*, Mark McGurl describes how American fiction has become inseparable from its institutional context – the university – as particularly embodied in the writing workshop. The book is remarkable in many respects, not least for McGurl's suggestive readings of a host of major American writers, not just Flannery O'Connor and Raymond Carver, the compact form and ashamed contents of whose work have made them program icons, but also verbally expansive writer-professors like Nabokov and Joyce Carol Oates. In terms of the intellectual history of the writing workshop, *The Program Era* marks a turning point, after which the MFA program comes to seem somehow different than it had previously seemed. It feels, reading McGurl, as if the MFA beast has at last been offered a look in the mirror, and may finally come to know itself as it is.

This may seem paradoxical, or backward: the writing program, after all, has long existed as an object of self-study for the people who actually attend such things, or teach in them, usually in the form of satire – David Foster Wallace's *Westward the Course of Empire*

Takes Its Way, Francine Prose's *Blue Angel*, that movie with the Belle & Sebastian soundtrack, and on and on. But (to borrow one of McGurl's many ideas) the program writer, even if he's been both student and professor, always wants to assume, and is to some extent granted, outsider status by the university; he's always lobbing his flaming bags of prose over the ivied gate late at night. Then in the morning he puts on a tie and walks through the gate and goes to his office. In the university, the fiction writer nevertheless managed not to think of himself as of the university.

McGurl interrupts this unself-consciousness by filing a full and official report from across the hallway: from the English Department proper, forcing the aspiring novelist to look across that hallway and notice a bunch of graduate students and professors sitting there, in identical offices, wielding identical red pens. You're like me now! is one of the cheerful subtexts of *The Program Era* – a literary critic's pointing-out that the creative writer is just as institutionally entangled as the critic has long been acknowledged to be. Or, more charitably put (for McGurl is perpetually charitable), that the fiction writer, at last, can cease fretting about how free and wild he is and get to work.

But what kind of work? One good outcome of McGurl's analysis would be to lay to rest the perpetual handwringing about what MFA programs do to writers (e.g., turn them into cringing, cautious, post-Carverite automatons). Because of the universitization of American fiction that McGurl describes, it's virtually impossible to read a particular book and deduce whether the writer attended a program. For one thing, she almost certainly did. For another, the workshop as a form has bled downward into the colleges, so that a writer could easily have taken a lifetime's worth of workshops as an undergraduate, à la Jonathan Safran Foer. And even if the writer has somehow never heard of an MFA program, or set foot on a college campus, it doesn't matter, because if she's read any American fiction of the past sixty years, or met someone who did, she's imbibed the general idea and aesthetic. We are all MFAs now.

On the flip side (as McGurl can't quite know, because he attended 'real' grad school), MFA programs themselves are so lax and laissez-faire as to have a shockingly small impact on students' work – especially shocking if you're the student, and paying $80,000 for the privilege. Staffed by writer-professors preoccupied with their own work or their failure to produce any; freed from pedagogical urgency by the tenuousness of the link between fiction writing and employment; and populated by ever younger, often immediately postcollegiate students, MFA programs today serve less as hotbeds of fierce stylistic inculcation, or finishing schools for almost-ready writers (in the way of, say, Iowa in the '70s), and more as an ingenious partial solution to an eminent American problem: how to extend our already protracted adolescence past 22 and toward 30, in order to cope with an oversupplied labor market.

Two years spent in an MFA program, in other words, constitute a tiny and often ineffectual part of the American writer's lifelong engagement with the university. And yet critics continue to bemoan the mechanizing effects of the programs, and to draw links between a writer's degree-holding status and her degree of aesthetic freedom. Get out of the schools and live! they urge, forgetting on the one hand how much of contemporary life is lived in the shadow of the university, even if beyond its walls; and on the other hand how much free living an adult can do while attending two classes per week. It's time to do away with this distinction between the MFAs and the non-MFAs, the unfree and the free, the caged and the wild. Once we do, perhaps we can venture a new, less normative distinction, based not on the writer's educational background but on the system within which she earns (or aspires to earn) her living: MFA or NYC.

There were 79 degree-granting programs in creative writing in 1975; today there are 854! This explosion has created a huge source of financial support for working writers, not just in the form of lecture fees, adjunctships, and temporary appointments – though these abound – but honest-to-goodness jobs: decently paid, relatively secure compared to other industries, and often even tenured. It would be fascinating to know the numbers – what percentage of the total income of American fiction writers comes from the university, and what percentage from publishing contracts – but it's safe to say that the university now rivals, if it hasn't surpassed, New York as the economic center of the literary fiction world. This situation – of two complementary economic systems of roughly matched strength – is a new one for American fiction. As the mass readership of literary fiction has peaked and subsided (it's always bracing to pick up an old Cheever or Updike paperback and see the book trumpeted as a #1 best-seller), and the march of technology sends the New York publishing world into spasms of perpetual anxiety, if not its much-advertised death throes, the MFA program has picked up the financial slack and then some, offering steady payment to more fiction writers than, perhaps, have ever been paid before.

Everyone knows this. But what's remarked rarely if at all is the way that this balance has created, in effect, two literary cultures (or, more precisely, two literary fiction cultures) in the US: one condensed in New York, the other spread across the diffuse network of provincial college towns that spans from Irvine to Austin to Ann Arbor to Tallahassee (with a kind of wormhole at the center, in Iowa City, into which one can step and reappear at the *New Yorker* offices on 42nd Street). The superficial differences between these two cultures can be summed up charticle-style: short stories vs. novels; Amy Hempel vs. Jonathan Franzen; library copies vs. galley copies; *Poets & Writers* vs. the *Observer*; *Wonder Boys* vs. *The Devil Wears Prada*; the

Association of Writers and Writing Programs (AWP) conference vs. the Frankfurt Book Fair; departmental parties vs. publishing parties; literary readings vs. publishing parties; staying home vs. publishing parties. But the differences also run deep. Each culture has its own canonical works and heroic figures; each has its own logic of social and professional advancement. Each affords its members certain aesthetic and personal freedoms while restricting others; each exerts its own subtle but powerful pressures on the work being produced.

Of course the two cultures overlap in any number of obvious ways, some of them significant. The NYC writer most likely earned an MFA; the MFA writer, meanwhile, may well publish her books at a New York house.

There are even MFA programs in New York, lots of them, though these generally partake of the NYC culture. And many writers move back and forth between the MFA and NYC worlds, whether over the course of a career, or within a single year. A writer like Deborah Eisenberg, who spends half the year in New York and half at the University of Virginia; whose early stories were published to acclaim in the *New Yorker* but who subsequently became known (or unknown) as a 'writer's writer' – that is, a workshop leader's writer; whose fiction, oddly, never appears anymore in New York–based magazines, but who writes frequently for *NYRB*, and publishes new books to raves from a variety of New York organs, shows in how many ways a writer can slip between these two cultures before winding up perfectly poised between them. And yet what's so striking is how distinct the cultures do in fact feel, and how distinctly they at least pretend to function. On the level of individual experience, each can feel hermetic, and the traveler from one to the other finds herself in an alien land. The fact that it's possible to travel without a passport, or to be granted dual citizenship, makes them no less distinct.

The model for the MFA fiction writer is her program counterpart, the poet. Poets have long been professionally bound to academia; decades before the blanketing of the country with MFA programs requiring professors, the poets took to the grad schools, earning PhDs in English and other literary disciplines to finance their real vocation. Thus came of age the concept of the poet-teacher. The poet earns money as a teacher; and, at a higher level of professional accomplishment, from grants and prizes; and, at an even higher level, from appearance fees at other colleges. She does not, as a rule, earn money by publishing books of poems – it has become almost inconceivable that anyone outside of a university library will read them. The consequences of this economic arrangement for the quality of American poetry have been often bemoaned (poems are insular, arcane, gratuitously allusive, et cetera), if poorly understood. Of more interest here is the economic arrangement proper, and the ways in which it has become that of a large number of fiction writers as well.

As the fiction writer-teacher becomes the norm, the fiction MFA also becomes an odd hybrid. On the one hand, MFA programs are still studio-based: luxuries of time during which both serious and dilettantish people can develop their artistic skills outside the demands of the market. In this way the programs aspire to a kind of immanent (and convenient) ideal; it doesn't matter whether the student publishes now or in ten years or never, whether her degree ever earns her a penny, as long as she serves her muse. On the other hand, as available teaching jobs multiply, MFA programs become increasingly preprofessional. They provide, after all, a terminal degree in a burgeoning field. And (the ambitious student rightly asks) why not enter that field straightaway? After all, there are actual jobs available for MFA holders, while the other humanities stagnate, and overall unemployment hovers around 10 percent.

Thus the fiction writer's MFA increasingly resembles the poet's old PhD; not in the rigors of the degree itself – getting an MFA is so easy – but in the way it immerses the writer in a professional academic network. She lives in a college town, and when she turns her gaze forward and outward, toward the future and the literary world at large, she sees not, primarily, the New York cluster of editors and agents and publishers, but rather a matrix of hundreds of colleges with MFA programs, potential employers all, linked together by

Poets & Writers, AWP, and summertime workshops at picturesque makeout camps like Sewanee and Bread Loaf. More links, more connections, are provided by the attractive, unread, university-funded literary quarterlies that are swapped between these places, and by the endowments and discretionary funds that deliver an established writer-teacher from her home program to a different one, for a well-paid night or week, with everybody's drinks expensed: this system of circulating patronage may have some pedagogical value, but exists chiefly to supplement the income of the writer-teacher, and, perhaps more important, to impress upon the students the more glamorous side of becoming – of aspiring to become – a writer-teacher.

For the MFA writer, then, publishing a book becomes not a primary way to earn money, or even a direct attempt to make money. The book instead serves as a credential. Just as the critic publishes her dissertation in order to secure a job on an ever tightening market, the fiction writer publishes her book of stories, or her novel, to cap off her MFA. There is an element of liberation in this, however complex; the MFA writer is no longer at the whim of the market – or rather, has entered a less whimsical, more tolerant market. The New York publishing houses become ever more fearful and defensive, battened down against the encroachments of other 'media' old and new and merely imagined – but the MFA writer doesn't have to deal with those big houses. And if she does get published by one, she doesn't need a six-figure advance. On the whole, independent and university presses (as for the poet and the critic) will do just fine. The MFA writer is also exempt from publicity, to a large extent – she still checks her Amazon ranking obsessively, as everyone does, but she can do so with a dollop of humor, and not as an inquiry into professional survival. Instead she enters into the professor's publish-or-perish bargain (which should probably be called teach-or-perish), in which the writing of future books, no matter how they sell, results in professional advancement and increasing security. Is this not artistic freedom, of a quiet and congenial sort? Could not books be written here in the university, all sorts of different books, that could never be written from within the narrow confines of the New York publishing world?

Yes, but. The MFA writer escapes certain pressures, only to submit to others. Early in her career, for instance, she is all in a rush to publish – first to place stories in the quarterlies, and then to get some version of her MFA thesis into print, by hook or by crook, in order to be eligible for jobs.

While the NYC writer might be willing to toil obscurely for a decade or more, nourishing herself with the thought of a big psychic and financial payoff that might never come, the MFA writer is not. She has no actual physical New York to cling to, no parties to attend; if her degree is finished but her book is not, she's purely a castout from the world in which she wishes to move. This can encourage the publication of slight and sometimes premature books, books that might give readers, and the writer herself, the wrong idea of what she can do.

Then, later in the career, comes the more obvious pressure not to publish at all – she has, after all, become a professor, and a professor gets paid to profess. One escapes the shackles of the corporate publishing apparatus only by accepting those of the departmental administration, and of one's students, at which point the tradeoff can come to seem like a bait and switch – although as the MFA system matures, its aspirants no doubt become more clear-eyed about what awaits them.

The MFA system also nudges the writer toward the writing of short stories; of all the ambient commonplaces about MFA programs, perhaps the only accurate one is that the programs are organized around the story form. This begins in workshops, both MFA and undergraduate, where the minute, scrupulous attentions of one's instructor and peers are best suited to the consideration of short pieces, which can be marked up, cut down, rewritten and reorganized, and brought back for further review. The short story, like the ten-page college term paper, or the twenty-five-page graduate paper, has become a primary pedagogical genre-form.

It's not just that MFA students are encouraged to write stories in workshop, though this is true; it's that the entire culture is steeped in the form. To learn how to write short stories, you also have to read them. MFA professors – many of them story writers themselves – recommend story collections to their students. MFA students recommend other collections to one another; they also, significantly, teach undergraduate creative writing courses, which are built almost exclusively around short works. In classes that need to divide their attention between the skill of reading and the craft of writing (and whose popularity rests partly on their lack of rigor), there's no time for ploughing through novels. Also, scores of colleges now have associated literary journals, which tend overwhelmingly to focus on the short story; by publishing in as many of these as possible, a young writer begins building the reputation that will eventually secure her a job as a teacher-writer, and an older writer sustains her CV by the same means.

Thus the names that reverberate through the MFA system, from the freshman creative writing course up through the tenured faculty, tend to be those of story writers. At first glance, this may seem like a kind of collective suicide, because everyone knows that no one reads short stories. And it's true that the story, once such a reliable source of income for writers, has fallen out of mass favor, perhaps for reasons opposite to that of the poem: if in the public imagination poetry reeks suspiciously of high academia – the dry, impacted arcana of specialists addressing specialists – then the short story may have become subtly and pejoratively

associated with low academia – the workaday drudg-
ery of classroom exercises and assignments. The poet
sublimates into the thin air of the overeducated PhD;
the story writer melts down into the slush of the composition department. Neither hits the cultural mark. A
writer's early short stories (as any New York editor will
tell you) lead to a novel, or they lead nowhere at all.

But there's a dialectical reversal to be found here, in
which the story/novel debate reveals itself to be just one
aspect of the MFA/NYC cultural divide, and in which
the story might even be winning. One of the clearest
signs of that divide is the way that different groups of
writers are read, valued, and discussed in the two different 'places' – one could, for instance, live a long full
life in New York without ever hearing of Stuart Dybek,
a canonical MFA-culture story writer who oversaw the
Western Michigan program for decades before moving on to Northwestern. A new Gary Shteyngart novel,
meanwhile, will be met with indifference at most MFA
programs. Entire such NYC and MFA rosters could
be named. In effect, parallel and competing canons
of contemporary literature have formed – and when
it comes to canon formation, New York, and therefore
the novel, may be at a disadvantage.

New York can't be excelled at two things: super-
stardom and forgetfulness. And so the New York
'canon,' at any given moment, tends to consist of a
few perennial superstars – Roth, DeLillo, Pynchon,
Auster – whose reputations, paradoxically, are secure

at least until they die, and beneath whom circulate an ever changing group of acclaimed young novelists – Joshua Ferris, Nicole Krauss, Rivka Galchen, Jonathan Safran Foer – and a host of midcareer writers whose names are magnified when they put out a book and shrink in between. Except at the very top, reputation in this world depends directly on the market and the publishing cycle, the reviews and the prizes, and so all except those at the very top have little reason to hope for a durable readership. The contemporary New York canon tends to be more contemporary than canon – it consists of popular new novels, and previous books by the authors of same.

The MFA canon works differently. The rapid expansion of MFA programs in recent decades has opened up large institutional spaces above and below: above, for writer-professors who teach MFA students; below, for undergraduate students who are taught by MFAs (and by former MFAs hired as adjuncts). All told, program fiction amounts to a new discipline, with a new curriculum. This new curriculum consists mainly of short stories, and the short fiction anthologies commonly used in introductory courses become the primary mechanism by which the MFA canon is assembled and disseminated.

A quick glance at some of the most popular anthologies shows the rough contours of the program canon. *The Vintage Book of Contemporary American Short Stories* (1994), edited by Tobias Wolff, honors the dirty realists and their successors, with a dedication to Raymond Carver, an introduction that begins, in classic dirty-realist fashion, 'A few years ago I met a wheat farmer from North Dakota . . . ,' and stories by Carver, Ann Beattie (University of Virginia), Richard Bausch (Memphis), Richard Ford (Trinity College, Dublin), Tim O'Brien (Texas State–San Marcos), and Jayne Anne Phillips (Rutgers), as well as Dybek (Northwestern), Joy Williams (Wyoming), Robert Stone (Yale), Mary Gaitskill (until recently, Syracuse), Barry Hannah (Mississippi, before his death), Ron Hansen (Santa Clara), Jamaica Kincaid (Claremont McKenna), Edward P. Jones (George Washington), Joyce Carol Oates (Princeton), Mona Simpson (Bard), Denis Johnson (currently unaffiliated), and Wolff's Stanford colleague John L'Heureux. *The Scribner Anthology of Contemporary Short Fiction* (2007) retains a dozen of Wolff's picks, and adds a new generation of post-dirty, ethnically diverse writers: Amy Bloom (Wesleyan), Peter Ho Davies (Michigan), Junot Díaz (MIT), et alia. Ben Marcus's *Anchor Book of New American Short Stories* (2004) rounds out the picture, overlapping with Scribner but not Vintage, adding still younger writers, and emphasizing recent contributions to the anti-dirty, explicitly stylized or stylish tradition, for instance Aimee Bender (USC), Gary Lutz (Pitt-Greenberg), and Mary Caponegro (Bard).

Via these anthologies – and via word of mouth and personal appearance – a large and somewhat stable body of writers is read by a large number of MFAs and an even larger number of undergrads, semester in and semester out. Thus the oft-scorned short story may secure a more durable readership than the vaunted novel. While Denis Johnson won a National Book Award in 2007 for his novel *Tree of Smoke*, and Junot Díaz a Pulitzer in 2008 for his novel *The Brief Wondrous Life of Oscar Wao*, these writers' reputations and readerships may rely more heavily on their single, slim volumes of stories, *Jesus' Son* and *Drown*, both of which are reliably anthologized and have entered the consciousness of a whole generation of college students.

One could even suggest that, in the absence of a contemporary American canon produced by the critics in the English department (that one consists only of Toni Morrison), the writers in the MFA program have gone ahead and built their own – as well as the institutional means to disseminate, perpetuate, and replenish it. This canon centers on short works, and distinguishes itself from the New York canon in other ways. While it still avails one to be a white guy in NYC, at least at the top of the market where Franzen, DeLillo, and Roth reside (and where the preferred ethnic other remains the Jewish male), the MFA canon has a less masculine tone, and a more overt interest in cultural pluralism. And while the New York list updates itself with each new copy of the *Times Book Review*, the MFA canon dates back, with pointed precision, to 1970 – the year of the earliest story in both the Vintage and Scribner anthologies. NYC remembers the '70s not at all, and the '80s only for the coke, but the MFA culture keeps alive the reputations of great (Ann Beattie), near-great (Joy Williams), and merely excellent writers whom publishing has long since passed by.

1970, not coincidentally, also marks the beginning of the careers of many of the eminent writers who emerged from the MFA heyday of the early '70s, and who now hold the most distinguished chairs in the MFA culture. Thus the MFA canon is a living canon not just by definition – it is after all 'contemporary' literature – but because the writers who comprise it are constant presences on the scene, and active shapers of the canon's contents. They teach (however reluctantly), they advise, they anthologize, they travel from program to program to read. A writer's university becomes an automatic champion of her work, and as her students disperse to jobs at other schools, so does the championing. The writer doesn't assign her own work – she doesn't have to – but she assigns that of her friends, and invites them to speak. It will be interesting to see what happens when this group of older writers dies (they are unlikely to give up their jobs beforehand); whether the MFA canon will leap forward, or back, or switch tracks entirely, to accommodate the interests, private and aesthetic, of a younger group of writer-teachers. Perhaps (among other possibilities) the MFA culture will take a turn toward the novel.

As the MFA fiction writer moves toward the poetic/

academic model, the NYC writer moves toward the Hollywood model. Not because fiction writers earn their keep as screenwriters (a few do, but that was by and large an earlier era; MFA/NYC could be said to have replaced NYC/LA as an organizing cultural rubric), but because New York publishing increasingly resembles the Hollywood world of blockbuster-or-bust, in which a handful of books earn all the hype and do humongous business; others succeed as low-budget indies; and the rest are released to a shudder of silence, if at all. Advances skew to the very high and the pitifully low, and the overall economics of the industry amplify and reinforce this income gap, as the blockbuster novelist not only sells her book to an actual film studio – thus stepping out of the shadow-world into the true bright one – but also parcels out lucrative translation rights to foreign markets. The advance multiplies; the money makes money. And – what's better than money – people will actually read the book.

Thus the literary-corporate publishing industry comes to replicate the prevailing economic logic, in which the rich get richer and the rest live on hope and copyediting. As with any ultracompetitive industry, like professional basketball or hedge funds, exceptional prestige accrues to the successes, and with some reason. The NYC writer has to earn money by writing (or else consider herself a failure in her own terms), which gives her a certain enlarged dignity and ambition. It also imposes certain strictures. First off, as already mentioned, it demands that the writer write novels.

Second, and perhaps most important, to be an NYC writer means to submit to an unconscious yet powerful pressure toward readability. Such pressure has always existed, of course, but in recent years it has achieved a fearsome intensity. On one hand, a weakened market for literary fiction makes publishing houses less likely than ever to devote resources to work that doesn't, like a pop song, 'hook' the reader right away. On the other, the MFA-driven shift in the academic canon has altered the approach of writers outside the university, as well as those within. Throughout the latter half of the last century, many of our most talented novelists – Nabokov, Gaddis, Bellow, Pynchon, De-Lillo, Wallace – carved out for themselves a cultural position that depended precisely on a combination of public and academic acclaim. Such writers were readable enough to become famous, yet large and knotty enough to require professional explanation – thus securing an afterlife, and an aftermarket, for their lives' work. Syntactical intricacy, narrative ambiguity, formal innovation, and even length were aids to canonization, feeding the university's need for books against which students and professors could test and prove their interpretive skills. Canonization, in turn, contributed to public renown. Thus the ambitious novelist, writing with one eye on the academy and the other on New York, could hope to secure a durable readership without succumbing (at least not fully) to the logic of the blockbuster. It was a strategy shaped by, and suited to, the era of the English department, which valued scholarly interpretation over writerly imitation, the long novel over the short story. (And when it came to white males imagining themselves into the canon, it helped that the canon was still composed mostly of white males.)

The death of David Foster Wallace could be said to mark the end of this quasi-popular tradition, at least temporarily. What one notices first about NYC-orbiting contemporary fiction is how much sense everyone makes. The best young NYC novelists go to great lengths to write comprehensible prose and tie their plots neat as a bow. How one longs, in a way, for endings like that of DeLillo's first novel, *Americana*, where everyone just pees on everyone else for no reason!

The trend toward neatness and accessibility is often posited to be the consequence of the workshop's relentless paring. But for NYC writers – despite their degrees – it might be better understood as the result of fierce market pressure toward the middlebrow, combined with a deep authorial desire to communicate to the uninterested. The NYC writer knows that to speak obliquely is tantamount to not speaking at all; if anyone notices her words, it will only be to accuse her of irrelevance and elitism. She doesn't worry about who might read her work in twenty years; she worries about who might read it now. She's thrown her economic lot in with the publishers, and the publishers are very, very worried. Who has both the money to buy a hardcover book and the time to stick with something tricky? Who wants to reread Faulknerian sentences on a Kindle, or scroll back to pick up a missed plot point? Nobody, says the publisher. And the NYC novelist understands – she'd better understand, or else she'll have to move to Cleveland.

It helps, too, to write long books; to address large-scale societal change and engage in sharp but affable satire of same; and to title the work with sweeping, often faintly nationalist simplicity: *Mason & Dixon*, say, or *American Pastoral* (*American* anything, really – *Psycho*, *Wife*, *Rust*, *Purgatorio*, *Subversive*, *Woman*). This is not to belittle these books, a few of which are excellent, but to point out that their authors are only partly at liberty (*American Liberty!*) to do otherwise. However naturally large the NYC novelist's imagination, it is shaped by the need to make a broad appeal, to communicate quickly, and to be socially relevant in ways that can be recreated in a review. The current archetype of this kind of novel also happens to be the best American novel of the young millennium – Jonathan Franzen's *Freedom*. (Franzen, famously, offered an unfortunately ahistorical account of the novelist's difficult relationship to difficulty in a 2002 essay about William Gaddis.) Having written, in *The Corrections*, a clear and lyrical long novel that brought large social and political forces to bear on domestic life, Franzen followed it with an even longer and clearer novel that brings even larger social and political forces to bear on domestic life. He could hardly have done anything else. *Freedom* is the most simply written of his books and also the most complex and best; it grapples with the most unspeakable of contemporary political problems – overpopulation – in a rivetingly plainspoken way. The novelist who converts heroic effort into effortless prose has been a standard figure since Flaubert, but in Franzen this project comes to seem like something else, something more momentous and telling if not aesthetically superior – something, perhaps, like the willed effort of the entire culture to create for itself a novel that it still wants to read.

In short, the writer who hopes to make a living by publishing – whether wildly successful like Franzen, more moderately so, or just starting out – is subject to a host of subtle market pressures, pressures that might be neutral in their aesthetic effects, but which enforce a certain consistency, and a sort of Authorial Social Responsibility. Regardless of whether reading comprehension and attention spans have declined, the publishers think that they have, and the market shapes itself accordingly. The presumed necessity of 'competing for attention' with other media becomes internalized, and the work comes out crystal-clear. The point is not that good books go unpublished – to the contrary, scores of crappy literary novels continue to get snapped up by hopeful editors. The point is that market forces cause some good books to go unnoticed, and even more – how many more? – to go unwritten.

And the NYC writer, because she lives in New York, has constant opportunity to intuit and internalize the demands of her industry. It could be objected that just because the NYC writer's editor, publisher, agent, and publicist all live in New York, that doesn't mean that she does too. After all, it would be cheaper and calmer to live most anywhere else. This objection is sound in theory; in practice, it is false. NYC novelists live in New York – specifically, they live in a small area of west-central Brooklyn bounded by DUMBO and Prospect Heights.

They partake of a social world defined by the selection (by agents), evaluation (by editors), purchase (by publishers), production, publication, publicization, and second evaluation (by reviewers) and purchase (by readers) of NYC novels. The NYC novelist gathers her news not from *Poets & Writers* but from the *Observer* and Gawker; not from the academic grapevine but from publishing parties, where she drinks with agents and editors and publicists. She writes reviews for *Bookforum* and the Sunday *Times*. She also tends to set her work in the city where she and her imagined reader reside: as in the most recent novels of Shteyngart, Ferris, Galchen, and Foer, to name just four prominent members of the *New Yorker*'s 20-under-40 list.

None of this amounts to a shrewd conspiracy, as mystified outsiders sometimes charge, but it does mean that the NYC writer participates in the publishing and

reviewing racket to an unnerving extent. She is an una-
bashed industry expert. Even if years away from fin-
ishing her first novel, she constantly and involuntarily
collects information about what the publishing industry needs, or thinks it needs. Thus the congeniality of
Brooklyn becomes a silky web that binds writers to the
demands of the market, demands that insinuate themselves into every detail and email of the writer's life.
It seems like a sordid situation. Then again, the publishing industry has always been singularly confused,
unable to devote itself fully to either art or commerce,
so perhaps the influence works both ways; perhaps the
NYC writer, by keeping the industry close, hopes also
to keep it honest, and a little bit interested in the art it
champions.

What will happen? Economically speaking, the
MFA system has announced its outsized ambitions,
making huge investments in infrastructure and personnel, and offering gaudy salaries and propitious
working conditions to secure top talent. The NYC
system, on the other hand, presents itself as cautious
and embattled, devoted to hanging on. And a business model that relies on tuition and tax revenue (the
top six MFA programs, according to *Poets & Writers*,
are part of large public universities); the continued
unemployability of 20-somethings; and the continued
hunger of undergraduates for undemanding classes,
does seem more forward-looking than one that relies on overflow income from superfluous books by

celebrities, politicians, and their former lovers. It was announced recently that Zadie Smith – one of the few writers equipped by fame to do otherwise – has accepted a tenured position at NYU, presumably for the health insurance; perhaps this marks the beginning of the end, a sign that in the future there will be no NYC writers at all, just a handful of writers accomplished enough to teach in NYC. New York will have become – as it has long been becoming – a place where some writers go for a wanderjahr or two between the completion of their MFAs and the commencement of their teaching careers. No one with 'literary' aspirations will expect to earn a living by publishing books; the glory days when publishers still waffled between patronage and commerce will be much lamented. The lit-lovers who used to become editors and agents will direct MFA programs instead; the book industry will become as rational – that is, as single-mindedly devoted to profit – as every other capitalist industry. The writers, even more so than now, will write for other writers. And so their common ambition and mission and salvation, their profession – indeed their only hope – will be to make writers of us all.

Kristin Dombek

– The Two Cultures of Life –

O n May 31, 2009, Scott Roeder walked into the Reformation Lutheran Church in Wichita and killed George Tiller, the abortion doctor, who was passing out bulletins for the morning service. Roeder put a .22-caliber pistol to Dr. Tiller's forehead, shot him point-blank, stood beside him until he collapsed, and then ran. In the days following the murder, we were told just enough about the killer to imagine him as a familiar kind of American character. He had been caught in the '90s with the makings of a bomb. He had been investigated by the FBI for connections to the Freeman movement. He subscribed to the right-wing newsletter Prayer and Action News. He drove a 1993 powder blue Ford Taurus. When he was captured, police found an envelope on the dashboard, on which was written the telephone number of Cheryl Sullenger, senior policy adviser for Operation Rescue, an anti-abortion group that had bombed clinics in the '90s. We were told that Roeder was most likely the author of an ominous post to Operation Rescue's website a few years ago, a post that read, in part, 'Bless everyone for attending and praying in May to bring justice to Tiller and the closing of his death camp.'

Dr. Tiller's clinic, Women's Health Care Services, was one of only three in the country where women with health- and life-threatening pregnancies could get late-term abortions. For more than two decades, it had been seen by pro-lifers as a site of genocide. In 2002, Operation Rescue's president, Troy Newman, had moved the organization's headquarters to Wichita to focus its full arsenal of direct action tactics on Tiller's clinic. For seven years, the group publicized the names and addresses of clinic workers, blanketed their neighborhoods with postcards of bloody fetuses, followed them around town in SUVs, paced with crosses on the sidewalks in front of their houses, and performed 'exorcisms' on their front lawns. Bill O'Reilly called the doctor 'Tiller the Baby Killer' when he excoriated the 'death mill' on his Fox News show, which he did during twenty-nine episodes from 2005 to 2009 – this according to the Daily Kos website, where clips are collected under the title 'O'Reilly's Jihad.' As Democratic pundits were eager to point out after the murder, Roeder's feelings about George Tiller's death camp were, among anti-abortion conservatives, common enough.

Even so, Roeder was called, by Kansans for Life president Mary Kay Culp, a 'lone nut,' and by his brother, 'crazy'; Operation Rescue president Troy Newman said Roeder had never been a member of the organization. Dr. James Dobson, the founder of Focus on the Family, was shocked by Roeder's 'act of vigilantism.' Charmaine Yoest, president and CEO of

Americans United for Life, said he wasn't even 'part of the pro-life movement.' On the left, many called him a 'terrorist' (Ben Schwartz in his Huffington Post blog: 'Where is the right-wing pro-torture faction when it comes to waterboarding a domestic terrorist who happens to be a right-wing American?'). Terrorists are always part of a cell, and numerous news sources picked up KMBC-TV's report that 'people often came and went from his house.' The more that conservatives disowned Roeder, the more liberals treated him as a symptom of Republican desires. 'Who'll be the next target of O'Reilly and Beck's ire,' worried Daily Kos's Markos Moulitsas on Twitter, 'to get gunned down by a domestic conservative terrorist?' But while the media and the blogosphere split into predictable camps over the question of whether Roeder was a lone vigilante or O'Reilly's pawn, everyone agreed on one thing: for a pro-lifer to murder an abortion doctor was the worst kind of hypocrisy, an obvious contradiction of the pro-life tenet that, as Charmaine Yoest put it, 'The foundational right to life . . . extends to everyone.'

In the same month that Roeder walked into Tiller's church with his gun, a Gallup poll found that, for the first time, a majority of Americans – 51 percent – identified themselves as pro-life. Twenty-three percent of respondents said they believed abortion should be illegal in all circumstances. If the rhetoric of major pro-life groups like National Right to Life is any indication, members of this majority are used to understanding abortion as murder. The most prominent and mainstream pro-life voices, including Dr. Dobson, frequently compare abortion to the Nazi holocaust. If pro-life activists are fighting what they genuinely believe to be genocide, 'hypocritical' is not exactly the right word for Roeder's violence. Rather, it has a chilling logic. Why not fight a holocaust with murder, if it means saving millions of lives? In fact, why don't more pro-lifers do what Roeder did?

Yet most of our 150 million plus pro-lifers don't even approve of the coercive tactics of Operation Rescue, much less believe that the engineers of the genocide – abortion doctors, med school instructors, the leaders of NOW and Planned Parenthood, and pro-choice politicians like Obama – should be assassinated. And if *Roe v. Wade* were overturned, what should be the penalty for getting, or performing, an abortion? In states where pro-life legislators have proposed abortion bans that would challenge *Roe v. Wade*, or passed 'trigger laws' that would go into immediate effect should *Roe v. Wade* be overturned, the penalties for doctors have been a fine or a prison sentence of a few years, and for their clients, nothing at all.

When activists like Roeder break the movement's rules, it reveals, for a moment, this uncomfortable contradiction between pro-life rhetoric and practice. It's tempting to think, then, that pro-lifers don't really mean it when they call abortion 'murder' and 'genocide.' I think they do, and that if we want to understand the way that abortion wedges US politics into an eternal binary opposition, we should assume that they do, that abortion is murder, for them, albeit a very particular kind of murder – not criminal, exactly, but religious. Abortion works, for pro-lifers, like a sacrifice, abhorred by its celebrants even as they depend on it for meaning.

I have a picture of myself with Dr. James Dobson, taken at a prayer breakfast the morning after the 1990 March for Life in Washington DC. It was like meeting the apostle Paul, and I was nervous. I remember waiting in line to shake his hand, fumbling my hands between pockets and hips, longing to fold far enough inside myself that no one could see me. When it was my turn, Dr. Dobson twinkled his gray eyes at me and said, 'Thank you for fighting for life.' In the picture he has his arm around me and we're both smiling happily. I am wearing a peach-and-white-striped rugby shirt, my brown hair is permed and hot-rollered, and my face is carefully made up to look like the face of some suburban girl. I was 17 and a freshman at Calvin College, a Christian Reformed school in Grand Rapids, Michigan, three hours away from the Indiana farm where I spent my high school years, and I was not a suburban girl. The new friends with whom I'd made the trip to Washington were. They were the grandchildren of Dutch immigrants and, like almost everyone at Calvin, blond and about six feet tall. Their rugby shirts had been purchased by their industrious, credit card bearing parents in the gleaming malls of Michigan. My family rarely went to the mall. It was part of 'the world' we were trying so hard to separate ourselves from that we didn't celebrate Christmas (too commercialized), watch TV (too blasphemous), go to elementary school (too brainwashing), or clean our house very often (somehow related). I treasured my superior faith, but by this point, I might have given up even that in exchange for the knowledge these girls had of how to keep your fingernails clean past noon. I don't remember much of the march, except my sign, which was red and in the shape of a stop sign and said STOP ABORTION NOW like everyone else's. I remember the face of one counter-protester knotted in anger as she leaned over a barricade on Constitution Avenue to shout at us as we marched toward the Supreme Court – or perhaps this is not a memory of what happened, but of what I feared would happen. We massed on the Ellipse behind the White House, half a million strong, or so we thought, though the *Washington Post* called it two hundred thousand the next morning. Thinking about abortion made me feel sick. Scott Roeder saw the same movies I did, I suppose, in different church basements: *The Silent Scream*, *Whatever Happened to the Human Race?*, *How Should We Then Live?* We must have the same images in our minds. Babies move down a conveyor belt, and when one comes down the line missing an arm, an inspector picks it off and throws it in a bin.

A thousand plastic baby dolls, black dolls and white ones, lie scattered on salt flats. The camera pans slowly along rows of laboratory cages holding white bunnies and white mice and then – human babies. Abortion, these films taught us, means treating humans like consumer products, or animals. It's symptomatic of an ideology that masquerades as liberating and humanistic but is really sadistic, part of a culture of death.

Sometimes, even now, I think of abortion and I am back on the farm in Indiana, woken by a nightmare in my narrow, blue-wallpapered bedroom: they're coming for us, because if the secular humanists want to kill unborn babies, they must want to take all our good lives away. Abortion meant all Christian children were going to be put in concentration camps, and I wondered if I would stand up for my beliefs when they put the gun to my head, or deny Jesus, as I had done once already in the swim team lockerroom when I was 12.

I don't think I talked about these feelings with my new friends, though I suspect they shared them. Like any ritual, an antiabortion protest involves, for the participants, all sorts of mundane concerns: where could we get soda, which boys at the march were cute, who had lip gloss, how many more speakers, and when would Sandi Patty come on. President George H. W. Bush spoke to the crowd, briefly, by telephone, his voice crackling and indecipherable in the crisp January air. Finally, Sandi Patty sang 'Via Dolorosa' and 'Upon This Rock,' I think, on a stage so far away she was only a blotch of a red dress. Transparent helium-filled balloons the size of houses were tethered to the lawn; in each balloon, suspended, was a colossal fetus, floating above us, the White House, and the Washington Monument, caught between earth and heaven in its plastic womb.

The trip from Michigan to Washington had cost only $25. The campus Right to Life chapter had bused some two hundred of us undergraduates to the march and put us up in hotels. Rumor was the money had come from a couple of wealthy Michigan executives: Amway cofounder Richard DeVos Sr. and Edgar Prince, founder of Prince Automotive, both major Republican Party funders and Bush family friends. DeVos and Prince sat on the Council for National Policy and gave millions to Calvin College, Focus on the Family, the National and Michigan Right to Life committees, and countless other conservative organizations and political candidates. It was these families who had managed to arrange for two hundred college students to meet the leader of the Christian world at a breakfast where we spread white cloth napkins on our laps and ate omelets and sweet pork sausage links and bacon on real china; we were, after all, the future.

In the moment that photograph with Dobson memorializes, I couldn't have imagined any way to be but pro-life, anything I wanted more than to fit in with the well-showered and glamorous world of mainstream evangelical Christianity. A year later, I wouldn't be caught dead in anything but flannel shirts; I'd stop washing my hair and give up the sausage and the bacon, stop eating meat at all. I declared myself a Marxist and joined a group that lobbied our school's administration to protect gay and lesbian faculty and students at the college. When I look at this photo now, it looks like I'm floating outside of time in that rugby shirt, standing next to a cardboard cutout of a famous man, suspended between conservatism and liberalism, Christianity and atheism, an Indiana childhood and an adulthood in which I would go east and find new victims to save and enemies to fear, though oddly it would always feel a little like fighting abortion did.

For me, what links veganism and antihomophobia and justice to abortion and what I learned from my childhood, is that if it looks like violence, it is violence. The necessary technological condition for the pro-life movement was the ultrasound machine, and it was right there on the screen: even at twelve weeks, the fetus recoiled from the suction curette. The scientific consensus was that this recoil was mere reflex, and that pain perception is impossible until the thalamus and cortex link, which begins to happen quite late in gestation. Until the mid-1980s, medical doctors didn't use anesthesia for surgery on prematurely born babies or even infants, because their cortexes weren't fully formed. Then a team of Oxford researchers, led by Dr. Kanwal Anand, produced evidence to argue that newborns do perceive pain, and revolutionized medical practice. Surgeons now regularly use anesthesia with newborns and preemies, who these days can survive outside the womb at twenty-one weeks. Anand argued in subsequent papers that consciousness is not necessary to pain perception, that even in the second trimester, fetuses have such highly concentrated nerve endings, and such undeveloped pain-inhibiting mechanisms, that they may feel pain particularly intensely. What 'consciousness' and 'perception' of pain mean is a matter of considerable scientific messiness – one most thoroughly researched and debated by the biologists, cognitive scientists, and psychologists who study pain in nonhuman animals.

But none of this mattered to us, because we could see it: the fetus opened its mouth in a silent scream. If it looks like violence, it is violence, and if it is violence, there's a system behind it, however hidden, and the system is evil, and should be fought against. This happens to be a worldview that travels.

—

First thing tomorrow, you are scheduled to be strapped down while an instrument with sharp metal teeth will clamp down on your foot and, with a twisting motion, pull it from your body. When the metal instruments are aimed at you, even the catchiest chant won't diminish the pain in your leg.

Then, without any anesthesia, your ankle and calf will be torn from your body to about your kneecap.

Then the thigh, then the other foot, calf and thigh pulled apart while you watch and scream in pain. But don't worry; the room is sound-proof and no one will be able to hear you. Oh, you're still alive. Bleeding, but not as much as you're going to be when your right hand is ripped off your wrist. Then your forearm, then all the way to your shoulder. And then the left hand and arm. Then your torso will be ripped apart, exposing your rib cage and beating heart. The heart will stop beating just about the time your head is crushed. That's what will happen from 9 to about 9:30 tomorrow morning.

Face it: Abortion makes Gitmo look like summer camp. And we've been torturing American children for 35 years now.

– Janet Porter, WorldNetDaily.com, January 22, 2008

These days, despite millions of exceptions, the battle lines are clearly drawn: to be pro-life is to be conservative, which implies – at least in the standard version – a number of other positions as unrelated (and even contradictory) as they are compulsory; if you're pro-life, you're likely to be for capital punishment, for example, and hunting, and meat-eating, and capitalism, and processed foods, and the right to drive an SUV. But it hasn't always been this way; at the birth of the culture wars, things were much more complicated.

In the '70s, my parents were long-haired, corduroy-bell-bottom-wearing, anti-authoritarian biblical literalists, proud to call themselves fundamentalist

Christians. They fought on the front lines of the battle to legalize homeschooling in Philadelphia not only to keep us free from the secular state's brainwashing, but so that they could make sure my brother and I ate an organic diet, learned at our own pace, and had plenty of time to freely explore all our artistic impulses. When I was 9, they moved us back to Indiana, where they had grown up, to live on a farm among the older generation of fundamentalists, our sweet grandmothers and their friends, who worried over the acceptability of pants and makeup, who never drank alcohol or danced. In the '70s and '80s, evangelicalism was in its own genera-tional battle over participation in 'secular' culture and politics, and it took abortion to unite us.

There are other ways to tell the story of the rise of the Christian Right in the '80s: it was a backlash against the sexual revolution and the use of abortion as birth control; it was about the greed of the televan-gelists, who built their audiences by prophesying the country's decline; it was about politics, the free-market Republicans using religious leaders as pawns to build a conservative base; it was about race and the Christian education movement, which came under threat when the IRS stripped tax-exempt funding from segregated Christian schools.

On the ground, however – at least among white evangelicals in the North (the Southern Baptists and the black church have their own histories) – what it felt like was an intellectual revolution. Those who were surprised by the rise of the religious right had missed what we were reading, because the *New York Times* and other newspapers didn't count Christian bookstores in their tallies. We were reading the Schaeffers, Francis and his wife, Edith, and their son, Franky – and most importantly, we were reading Francis Schaeffer's *A Christian Manifesto*, which argued that we should use political involvement and civil disobedience to fight against an increasingly totalitarian secular state, and *How Should We Then Live?*, which argued that we should reclaim the West's great art and literature, and find our Christian worldview there.

My parents idolized the Schaeffers, and so did I. They lived in a château in Switzerland called L'Abri, which was a sort of commune, way station, and think tank for anyone interested in talking seriously about theology, whether that was students backpacking Europe or leaders of the emerging Christian Right. The Schaeffers championed art and music and intellectual arguments for 'fundamentalist' views, lending a boho European cool to conservative Christian positions. So when they told us to fight abortion, it meant fighting human authority; abortion became – and still is, for millions of conservatives – the Man.

In the late '70s, they came to the States on a world tour, with their ten-episode film series *How Should We Then Live?*, which played Madison Square Garden and other civic auditoriums around the country. The first eight episodes were about philosophy and art history, and the last two episodes were about abortion. And then they came back, in 1980, which is when I saw them, as a child; I remember Edith's soft admonishments about building Christian homes, and her son Franky's angry, stage-pacing tirades about how we had to improve the quality of Christian art. This time they brought the five-episode pro-life film series *Whatever Happened to the Human Race?*, which gave us the images I described above: the baby dolls on the assembly line, scattered on salt flats, and caged in laboratories like animals. With narration by Francis Schaeffer and C. Everett Koop (then surgeon-in-chief at the Children's Hospital of Philadelphia, soon to become surgeon general), the films persuaded us that abortion was a first step toward state-run infanticide and euthanasia. Part of one episode was shot at Auschwitz; another, with the blessing of the Israeli government, at Yad Vashem. It was easy to see how slippery was the slope from *Roe v. Wade* to National Socialism.

As Franky Schaeffer later argued in his 2007 book *Crazy for God*, fighting abortion is not in its essence conservative; at a certain point in the late 1970s, it could have been taken up by social progressives instead. Before the Schaeffers, Protestant Christians didn't care much about abortion; it was a Catholic issue. Planned Parenthood, until 1968, called abortion the killing of human life, while the Southern Baptists advocated for abortion's legality until 1980. But through their films, their seminars, and their books, the Schaeffers told conservative evangelicals – and James Dobson, Jerry Falwell, Pat Robertson, everyone listened – that abortion was our issue, and that it meant the apocalypse of our values. As Dr. Dobson put it in a 2002 speech, 'Thank God for Francis Schaeffer. He saw everything we're going through today. He laid it all out.'

For much of the last century, the American left fought for the rights of those without voices, those considered not fully human: for women, African-Americans, workers, gays and lesbians, immigrants. It is usually those on the left, still, who fight for the rights of another set of beings that haunt the edges of the human: the animals who provide us with companionship, entertainment, and food. Yet the belief that fetuses shouldn't be subjected to involuntary termination, and the belief that animals shouldn't be tortured and killed for human consumption, occupy positions that could not be more distant from each another in our contemporary cultural landscape.

—

Imagine you are strapped to a table. Your gut instinct is to trust the people around you. You are in their care. But your body begins to burn. Behind you, muddled words escalate with the same fury as the scalded skin you cannot reach. You are afraid.

They seem indifferent to your now blood-splattered limbs. That morning, you'd dreamed about a walk and food. But today you are their research. Their data is your response-pain, boundless and unrelent-ing. As they blind, burn and inject poison into your exhausted body, you wonder: why?

In the Draize test chemicals are poured into the clipped-open eyes of restrained animals. Many break their necks or backs trying to escape. Reactions in-clude swollen eyelids, inflamed irises bleeding, massive deterioration and blindness. For Draize skin irritancy tests, abrasive chemicals seep into the shaved skin of immobilized animals. To expose skin, adhesive tape is repeatedly stripped off an animal's body. After every test animals are killed and analyzed.

– Brenda Shoss, 'Must Mascara and Soap Hurt
This Much?,' www.kinshipcircle.org

When Scott Roeder murdered George Tiller, the only US citizen on the FBI's Most Wanted Terrorists list was Daniel Andreas San Diego, who was allegedly in-volved in the 2003 bombings of three Bay Area office buildings belonging to the Chiron and Shaklee Corpo-rations, customers of the animal testing lab Hunting-ton Life Sciences. Huntington's employees have been caught on tape doing things like punching puppies and dissecting monkeys alive. According to the FBI's website, San Diego has 'psychopathic' tattoos of burn-ing hills and collapsing buildings. He has 'ties to ani-mal rights extremist groups' and is 'known to follow a vegan diet, eating no meat or food containing animal products.' No one was hurt in the Bay Area bombings – they caused only property damage – and San Diego is only a suspect; nevertheless, he is still, at this writing, at the top of the FBI's list.

How did a person not convicted but suspected of committing a nonviolent offense that caused property damage in the name of preventing illegal cruelty against animals become the first American citizen to be placed on the FBI's Most Wanted Terrorists list? Antiabortion activists like Roeder and the members of Operation Rescue weren't included, at the time of Roeder's murder, in the FBI website's definition of domestic terrorism, which read: 'Today's domestic terror threats run the gamut, from hate-filled white supremacists . . . to highly destructive eco-terrorists . . . to violence-prone anti-government extremists . . . to radical separatist groups.' In our country's binary politics, 'domestic terrorists' are often defined by the party in power, and are in turn scapegoated by that party. But San Diego's story is more complicated.

During the Bush era, 'eco-terrorists' and animal rights activists were framed as our most dangerous local threat. After 9/11, the FBI took advantage of new leeway to infiltrate not just organizations like the Arab Anti-Defamation League, but Greenpeace and PETA. A 2005 report by the ACLU showed the FBI had expanded its definition of 'terrorism' to include groups that fight environmental crime and animal cruelty. The FBI, revealed the report, had infiltrated a number of animal rights groups, using PETA interns as spies and conducting surveillance on such seemingly innocuous activities as the distribution of 'vegetarian starter kits' in Indiana. The Animal Enterprise Terrorism Act, passed in early 2006, expanded the FBI's powers of interdiction: any 'force, violence, and threats involving animal enterprises,' any 'interference' in an 'animal enterprise,' or any 'conspiracy to interfere' became terrorism, and punishable as such.

Soon after Obama took office, his administration was careful to reframe our fear, designating 'right-wing extremists' as the next great danger. In April 2009, a widely circulated Homeland Security document titled 'Right-Wing Extremism: Current Economic and Political Climate Fueling Resurgence in Radicalization and Recruitment' focused attention on antiabortion activists, as well as on white supremacists likely to react against our first African-American president, and returning veterans angry at the government that had trained them to kill. Conservative pundits and Republicans in the House and Senate complained of political profiling, and then the FBI, in what some have speculated was a compensatory move emblematic of the new administration's efforts to bridge the political poles, put its first domestic terrorist on the 'Most Wanted Terrorist' list – Daniel San Diego.

In this way, antiabortion and animal rights activists have served, in recent years, as exchangeable scapegoats, designated as terrorists according to the administration's needs and the media's next story. Roeder killed a man, leaving behind a grieving family and women with life-threatening pregnancies who had nowhere to go, while San Diego allegedly caused some property damage, and hurt no one. It doesn't matter. Once they are terrorists, activists are turned into players in an apocalyptic showdown between good and evil, and presidential administrations, the FBI, Fox News, and wealthy families from Grand Rapids argue over which characters belong in which narrative slots. This cataclysmic battle looks different depending on which side you're on, but what's dangerous about it, no matter where we stand, is its religious power to make us feel helpless and victimized by the players on the opposite side.

The last thing the apocalypse show wants us to ask is why the 'terrorists' do what they do. Roeder may well be mentally ill, and San Diego's own story is as mysterious as his position on the Most Wanted list. But the story of Ingrid Newkirk, who started PETA, is so well known as to be scripture among animal rights activists. Newkirk was born in England but spent her childhood in New Delhi, volunteering with her mother and Mother Teresa among the lepers. She moved to the US and one day in 1972, when she was 22, she took a litter of abandoned kittens to a shelter, where a woman thanked her and told her she would 'put them down.' Being British, Newkirk didn't understand the phrase, and found out only later, when she came back to visit the kittens, that they were dead. She felt she had betrayed them. She looked around: the living conditions were terrible, and the shelter animals were being killed in a back room. Newkirk had been studying to be a stockbroker, but she quit and took a job at the shelter, where she tried to improve the conditions in which the animals lived and died. After she saw the way the workers kicked them and stepped on them and shoved them into freezers, she started coming in early in the morning to euthanize them herself. 'I could always imagine myself,' she says in the HBO documentary *I Am an Animal*, 'going through what they were going through.'

Newkirk founded PETA with a friend, Alex Pacheco, in 1980; it was a few hippies meeting in a living room, she's fond of saying, until the case of the Silver Spring monkeys drew them into the national spotlight. Working undercover in the primate research lab of Dr. Edward Taub in Silver Spring, Maryland, Pacheco shot footage of living conditions that the National Institute of Health would later deem 'grossly unsanitary.' He also managed to catch on videotape Dr. Taub's experiments. Macaque monkeys were clamped by the neck, wrists, and ankles to a scaffolding, their arms spread wide, and – after nerves to their extremities were cut – they were dehydrated, starved, and then shocked. They looked like monkey crucifixes, and PETA displayed their pictures everywhere they could, with the slogan THIS IS VIVISECTION. Police raided the lab and Dr. Taub was charged with animal cruelty. PETA launched a ten-year lawsuit, and in the end, Dr. Taub's lab was shut down, he couldn't get a job, and there was a new amendment to the Animal Welfare Act that dictated standards for the care of laboratory animals. Like antiabortion activists, with their photos of bloody and dismembered fetuses, PETA had found its strategy: to show us the mutilated bodies that represent the suffering we'd rather ignore.

For my father, who taught me to venerate the Schaeffers and fear and fight abortion, it was the suffering body of Jesus that he wanted to make us see. He argued, whenever he got the chance, that we didn't focus enough on the cross. He had a seminary degree and was sometimes a guest preacher at local churches, and when I was in junior high and high school, his favorite sermon narrated the medical details of the crucifixion, down to the minute, or so it felt. He had been a Shakespearean actor before God called him to go to seminary, and he would boom out the description in a deep, ominous voice. Covered in bruises and cuts from his beating and whipping at the hands of the Roman legionnaires, bleeding from the scalp under his crown of thorns, dizzy and nauseated, raw-kneed from falling under the weight of the crossbeam on the Via Dolorosa, Jesus is nailed to the cross through his wrists (not his palms, my father said, as we know from the Shroud of Turin), and it begins: the muscles of his body cramp in turn, his breathing becomes shorter and shorter, he begins to asphyxiate from the weight of his body hanging off his arms. He must push himself up with the nails through his feet so that he can breathe enough to talk: Father, forgive them, for they know not what they do.

The sermon lasted an eternity, but no one walked out. My father was standing on a prosthetic leg; he had inched his way to the pulpit from his wheelchair with the help of two church elders. He had diabetes and epilepsy; he had, in recent years, contracted hepatitis C, acute pneumonia, staph infections; soon, he would have colon cancer and hemorrhages in his brain. The doctors did not know anyone with so many diseases, or why he was still alive. They'd been cutting his leg off, a piece at a time; his body was dying while he lived in it. He did not think we focused enough on the suffering body of Jesus, and what could we do but listen?

My mother became a full-time nurse to my father when she was in her early 30s. By the time she was 40 and I was in junior high, he was bedridden most of the time. Sometimes in the afternoons he spent hours on the couch, under an afghan. We did our chores, fed the animals, took turns bringing him his insulin shots and water for his pills, carried his urinal to the bathroom to empty it in the toilet. In the evenings, my mother took long walks away from the house, down the lane and across the fields, following hedgerows and the stream to the back woods, where we could not see her. I suspect she stood out there looking at the lights of the house from afar, as I would do later when I visited home from college or from New York – trying to wrap her head around it, see it differently somehow, fascinated and repelled, wishing she could keep walking. When she came back, she was quiet and red-eyed.

Every once in a while, my mother, brother, and I killed a few of our chickens for food. We strung them up by their feet from a tree behind the brooder house and hacked off their heads with machetes. They would flutter around for a while, not yet knowing they were dead, their blood emptying into the ground. We untied them, reached our hands inside to pull out their still warm organs, careful not to break the sack of bile that would poison the meat. Then we plucked out their feathers, held their bodies over the stove burners to singe off the stubble, and dropped them in pots of boiling water to cook.

Recently, I watched footage from undercover PETA investigations of scientific labs and slaughterhouses. A few seconds of monkeys bound and beaten, a grainy clip of a slaughterhouse employee laying into a pig with a tire iron, and I was, to my surprise, shaking with sobs so sudden and loud that I scared the cats. This is the problem of thinking you've witnessed a secret and malicious violence beneath the surface of your society: either you're crazy for caring so much about beings who everyone thinks are something less or other than human, or the world is crazy that would allow their systematic torture and death. Does this one pain matter, in a world of pain? Whose pain is this, anyway? And how can I bear to witness it alone?

It must be how my father felt, watching the doctors cut his body apart, and why he needed to make us concentrate, really concentrate, on every medical detail of Jesus' suffering and death, because how could he ask us to understand his own? It's what I felt, as a child, when I watched *The Silent Scream*'s ultrasound footage of a fetus recoiling from a suction curette, before fighting abortion became a way to leave the dirt of the farm behind, and then vegetarianism became a way to leave Jesus, like smoking was, and being pro-choice, and wearing flannel shirts instead of rugby shirts, at least until rugby shirts became hip again, in my Brooklyn neighborhood, but only if worn as an ironic nod to the adolescence that follows my generation like a shadow.

And if Ingrid Newkirk had been born in Wichita instead of England, and baptized in some church there, not Dr. Tiller's Reformed Lutheran Church, but say the Wichita Assembly of God, and if her parents taught her to believe that all human life is valuable, from conception on, would she have started PETA, or would she have started Focus on the Family? And if I had been born in England, and hung out with Mother Teresa and Hindus instead of learning to kill chickens in Indiana, in the shadow of the abortion apocalypse, would I still see, in a monkey vivisection or a slaughterhouse beating, the blood of the Lamb? Or was it Jesus, anyway, who Newkirk saw in the Silver Springs monkeys, their arms spread out and clamped onto metal crosses while lab technicians shocked them with electric prods?

What's radical in evangelical Christianity is the idea that it is no longer the job of the believer to do rituals, to strive for perfection; you don't need to slaughter a lamb, or count rosary beads, or lay oblations at an altar, or keep a candle burning, or chant Sanskrit phrases, or hate yourself for all your failures. The work is already done: Jesus has done it, once and for all, on the cross. To accept this revolutionary divine love is to be born again. This is what all the hoopla is about. When you're born again it's as if you had been accidentally living with your face planted in the dirt, thinking that was everything, and someone ever so quietly picked you up and just rolled you over so you could see the sky.

But there is a problem. By having God himself perform the sacrifice, rather than demand it from believers, Christianity tries to end violence, but it does so by displacing it from believers' everyday rituals to the virtual: the work is done, but you experience it all day long. A single person can identify with multiple roles in the same day. When I sin, I crucify him. When I suffer, I am on the cross with him, and he is with me; he has been to hell and back on my behalf. When I ask forgiveness for my failures, I am resurrected. When I see someone being hurt, I see Christ. When I help someone who is in pain, I ease Christ's suffering – and yet I need him there, on the cross, again and again, to redeem me.

The cross is a meaning machine. When your suffering is mundane – when your job or your family or your church or your country's politics or the doctors are taking pieces of you, bit by bit – it makes sense of things for you. But it also shocks you into living at a higher pitch. Some people, like my father – and Mel Gibson, whose movie about Jesus my father would have loved – become addicted. There is a whole field of crucifixion studies, conducted by men, for the most part, and a few women, who study the 'science' of the passion. The best known is a 1953 book by Pierre Barbet, A Physician at Calvary. 'When a surgeon has meditated on the sufferings of the Passion,' wrote Barbet, 'when he has worked out its timing and its physiological circumstances, when he has methodically set himself to reconstruct all the stages of that martyrdom of a night and a day, he can . . . as it were share in the sufferings of Christ.'

In 1995, Frederick T. Zugibe, a pathologist at Columbia University, carried out experiments to test Pierre Barbet's hypotheses that Jesus was nailed through the wrists and that he died of asphyxiation. Zugibe had a wooden cross constructed, strapped human volunteers to it with specially constructed leather gauntlets, and outfitted them with an electronic blood pressure unit and an ear oximeter probe to keep track of oxygen in the blood. Volunteers stayed on the cross for as long as they could, which was never more than forty-five minutes. Their hands and shoulders would cramp, or they would feel 'chest rigidity' or leg cramps, and Zugibe would let them down. No one had trouble breathing, and in this way Zugibe gathered evidence to show that Jesus, therefore, did not die of asphyxiation, but of traumatic and hypervolemic shock. If Zugibe was right, my father was wrong; the question, of course, is why it matters.

Unlike Zugibe's volunteers, and unlike Jesus, Dr. Taub's similarly strapped, tortured, and examined monkeys did not have a choice, which is Ingrid Newkirk's point; neither, of course, do fetuses, when they are poisoned or snapped into pieces and sucked out of a womb, and neither would women, should *Roe v. Wade* be overturned and they are forced to bear babies they do not want, or to risk their lives bringing problem pregnancies to term. This is the deep sacrificial drama of what or who can be forcibly made to suffer for a larger good, which keeps us mirroring each other across the divide.

My father did not die until I was 26 and in graduate school. My mother married again two years later, to a retired machinist who drove a school bus, and who woke early every morning to read the Puritans – a few pages of 'Sinners in the Hands of an Angry God,' say, before breakfast – and had a temper. The first time she left him, a couple of years ago, she went to a women's shelter. When she called to tell me, I flew to Indiana and checked into the Days Inn. We met at Ruby Tuesday, where the salad bar was, as she promised, real good. In our booth after the first trip to the buffet, my mother told me that she had looked in the phone book for the shelter's phone number while he was driving his afternoon school bus route, packed her bags and hid them in a closet, and drove away in the middle of the night, after pretending she couldn't sleep. I watched her carefully, because she was using her bouncy little girl voice as she told me this. She wore her long, straight hair parted down the middle, like the hippie she once was. She was tired, but she seemed kind of elated, said that the women at the shelter felt like the friends she's never had.

'My roommate? I love her. I just love her. She's been so kind to me.' This was for my benefit; neither my mother nor I think I'm kind enough to her. She leaned over her plate of ranch dressing doused lettuce and cucumbers and macaroni salad. 'Her husband?' she whispered. 'He tried to crucify her.'

There are sentences that tear a hole in the world with their impossibility, like the sentence on your voice mail in which your mother says she's been living in a shelter for battered women. After a sentence like that, it takes some time to piece the world together again. 'He tried to crucify her' was not that kind of sentence, but its opposite: the kind that feels like the inevitable punch line of a long joke that unlocks the secret logic of the world, or at least of Indiana, or maybe it's only our Indiana, my mother's and mine.

'He did not.'

'He did.

'He really did.'

I couldn't help smiling. Then we were both giggling. She was probably thinking: there's marriage for you. I was thinking: a Hoosier hears in church that a person nailed to a cross can take your sins away. He starts looking at his wife funny, makes a trip to the Ace Hardware. She hears his hammer clanging away behind the barn, and before she can put two and two together, he asks if she wants to go for a walk. The joke starts differently for my mother; for her, there's no questioning the logic of Jesus' crucifixion. But the punch line is the same.

It is not funny, what happened to this woman. Before she got away, my mother told me, he had managed to cut holes into her hands with a knife, to make it easier to get the nails through. He had seriously lost the script; we do not sacrifice grown-up humans, not anymore, not literally. But he may well have been reading his Bible, in which the most important stories are about someone willing to kill a family member because of God's demand. There is not only Abraham on Mount Moriah, knife raised over his son's bound body, but God himself, watching his Son whipped and nailed to the cross. If you're a Trinitarian, as most evangelicals are, this story hurts the mind. Look at it one way, and God the Father takes Jesus' life in exchange for us, to take our sins away, a conventional scapegoat demanded by a conventional asshole divinity. Look at it another way, and since Jesus is God incarnate, the crucifixion signifies the divinity's loving willingness to enter into human culture and play by our rules, giving himself on our behalf, in a gorgeous model of self-sacrifice that good Christians try to imitate every day.

But from this perspective, since God's son is a part of himself and therefore living inside him more like a fetus, really, than a child, the crucifixion is basically a divine abortion. Why not then see human abortion as a kind of self-sacrifice that imitates and honors God's? Perhaps Christian pro-lifers are less comfortable than they might think with their religion's central sacrificial story; no one, except the one guy in Indiana, really wants to be responsible for putting someone on a cross. Maybe it is for this reason that they alternately abhor and rehearse, fascinated, the story of the baby poisoned, disarticulated, sucked out, by doctors playing God, at the whim of a parent whose desires, to that helpless suffering being, are so mysterious as to be divine.

Even if we cannot agree on when a fetus transforms into a baby, or what kind of animal – human, monkey, horse, dog, chicken, rat, cockroach? – is a being worth saving from suffering, we can at least reflect on why a person transforms from one worldview to another, and why we treat each other as if this never happens. How many of us keep the same beliefs our whole lives, or even for two years in succession? Sometimes people are the most vehement about their take on the world when they're just about to change. We only ever find each other on our way to somewhere else.

In a pregnancy crisis center in Colorado Springs, while making a documentary theater piece with the playwright Stephen Wangh, I interviewed six anti-abortion counselors, all of them women whose activist work was motivated, at least in part, by their own prior abortions. At another point in their lives, they believed abortion was OK at least for them, at least right then. One of them was from Wichita. In the picture I took with my mind, she is a beautiful 24-year-old white woman with full lips and long brown hair, dressed in a black Adidas sweat suit with white piping. She sits with her legs gracefully tucked under her on a mauve couch in the back of the center, and talks carefully into my tape recorder. When she was a child, she begged her father to let her go to protests at Tiller's clinic. She imagined it as a butcher's shop, and always pictured Tiller with a meat cleaver. When she was 18, she got pregnant, and because she could not tell her Christian family that she had done the worst sin, sex before marriage, and because she wanted to go to med school, and have a life – because, she thinks now, she was selfish – she went to Tiller's clinic to have an abortion. They gave her tea and crackers; it astounded her how kind they all were. She wanted to tell her family and her friends, the protesters outside: Dr. Tiller is the nicest guy in the world!

A year later, she spent forty days fasting and praying, repenting the murder she had done, and now she tries to help pregnant mothers make the better decision; she's dedicated her life to 'telling the truth in love.' She'd studied at the Focus on the Family Institute, where they staged college campus protests with ten-foot pictures of aborted fetuses. She didn't like it at all. I asked her why, if abortion is murder, if we are in the middle of a genocide, they shouldn't use the most shocking tactics possible, or even bomb clinics, murder doctors. She paused, said she had thought about this a lot. But she'd come to believe that it wasn't worth the trauma to postabortive women. Her answer, in the end, was a feminist one: it was about not stigmatizing women for what they had done. In the moment this snapshot captures, she is an antiabortion activist. But she may be on her way to something else.

All the counselors talked of having their abortions in order not to disappoint or anger some male figure – their boyfriend, their husband, their father, their god. Some of them spoke of the shame of having sex outside of marriage in a Christian environment; abortion was a way out of being called a whore. They saw their pro-life activism as a way to help women make their own decisions, take charge of their own bodies, stop looking for approval in the arms of men; what they didn't see was what felt so clear, to me, listening to their stories – that without Christianity, they might not have felt such shame about sex, or such veneration for men, or such fear that they would never be accepted by their families and friends if they admitted to being sexually active. If it weren't for Christianity, they might not have had to kill their babies at all.

Without the right to choose abortion, these women wouldn't have been able to weigh sacrifice against sacrifice for themselves, and contingency against contingency, and I'll vote for that right forever. All I am saying is that this weighing is similar to the weighing we do when we consider the lives and deaths of animals, more similar than our current political landscape allows us to acknowledge. That doesn't mean the answers are the same; in fact, I think the two ethical problems are more heterogeneous than the polemics allow. At best, this weighing is not some calculus of suffering, the measuring of pain as if pain were countable, as if it were not endless. We can't even measure our own pain, much less the pain of others, particularly others who can't speak. Better to ask, of every act that causes suffering for a larger good, whether it's a kind of sacrifice we're willing to be responsible for, or if we're causing (or letting happen, from a distance) a violence that we don't want to look at. And to ask, too, when we feel overwhelming sentimental grief about something that looks like violence, whose suffering we're seeing there.

It's easy to call it deferral, when others do it – the self-concern that slides onto the fetus or nonhuman animal who cannot speak and can therefore articulate one's own victimization. Such substitution is at the heart of sacrifice, whose magical rituals allow us to abhor the suffering of others at the same time as we depend on the sense it makes of our lives, which begin and end in pain and contain plenty in the middle. And who hasn't felt helpless, at some point, in the face of some machine (a school, a church, a marriage, an office, a hospital, a factory farm, an economic system) that reproduces in us gender and health and even humanness itself, even as it cuts us apart. To fantasize about such helplessness, to become addicted to it, to love too much its drama: this temptation is hardly the sole province of Republicans or Democrats. And at the same time, when someone empathizes with the object of a medical procedure or a slaughter on a factory farm, the disarticulation of a body in a hidden place, and says, Enough, bring this violence into the light – there is something hopeful in that impulse, as well.

And so it's not enough to vote for choice, and deplore pro-lifers, though it's easy to do so, thanks in part to the reprehensible violence of activists like Roeder. For pro-choice progressives and animal rights sympathizers, demonizing pro-lifers is a good way to ignore the mirror they hold up to our own best and worst impulses, but a really bad way to accomplish our goals. If fighting abortion is, in part, a way for conservatives to be liberal, and defend the powerless and voiceless against the Man, then to ignore this common goal is to misunderstand them completely. And if fighting abortion is, in part, about projecting one's own experience of victimization onto the fetus, then ostracizing prolifers is not fighting for choice at all.

The same day he murdered Dr. Tiller, Scott Roeder was arrested on I-35; he'd made it only an hour and a half north of Wichita. You can watch the arrest on YouTube. Roeder was docile and cooperative; he even managed to get onto his knees while keeping his hands in the air, which looks difficult. But once he was cuffed and frisked and asked to get into the squad car, he started complaining. 'How in the heck – my legs are way too long. I could lay down, maybe, but I can't get my legs in there with my arms back here . . . I can't get in there.' From the Sedgwick County Jail, he called the Associated Press. He wanted us to know that he appreciated our prayers, and that there were 'many other similar events planned around the country as long as abortion remains legal.' But mainly, he wanted to complain about the 'deplorable conditions in solitary': the food was bad, the bed was hard, he hadn't been allowed enough phone calls, he didn't get his sleep apnea medicine, it was too cold. 'I started having a bad cough,' he told the AP. 'I thought I was going to have pneumonia.' He was being treated, he said, 'like a criminal.' Ingrid Newkirk seems better at imagining what martyrdom feels like these days; sometimes, during street protests, she spends hours in a cage, on purpose.

After the murder, Tony Newman, the president

of Operation Rescue, couldn't sleep for two days, and then he couldn't get out of bed at all. The Tiller family closed down the clinic; now you can't get a legal abortion within five hundred miles of Wichita. Seven years after Newman moved to Wichita to shut the clinic down, it was over. Newman called his inability to get out of bed 'abortion fatigue.' He had built his life around fighting Tiller; what would he do without the death camp?

The PETA lawsuits against Dr. Taub began in 1981 – one year after I saw the Schaeffers speak in Philadelphia – and ended in 1990, about the time I was marching for life in Washington. PETA wanted to take the monkeys to a sanctuary, but the Supreme Court rejected their application. Instead, the monkeys were euthanized and dissected by a team of NIH researchers, who discovered that the monkeys' brains had reorganized themselves to learn to move their paralyzed limbs. Neuroplasticity: one of the most important, and hopeful, scientific discoveries of the 20th century. Dr. Taub was allowed back into the lab, and started developing innovative ways to train human stroke victims, like the macaques, to remake their brains and their nervous systems, so that they could move dead limbs again. Thanks to the Silver Spring monkeys, we now know that brains can change; at any age, we can rebuild them.

Franky Schaeffer's in his 50s now, and he goes by Frank. He is still pro-life, but he's remade himself into a progressive, attends a Greek Orthodox church, and spends his time writing and traveling the country, telling his story. In 2008, he campaigned energetically for Obama. In 2009, he was the only one who claimed Roeder. In his regular Huffington Post blog, he wrote a post titled 'How I (and Other 'Pro-Life' Leaders) Contributed to Dr. Tiller's Murder.' In it he said, 'My father and I would have been shocked that someone took us at our word, walked into a Lutheran Church and pulled the trigger on an abortionist. But even if the murderer never read Dad's or my words we helped create the climate that made this murder likely to happen.'

I met Frank Schaeffer a few years ago; I wanted to get his story for the play. It had been more than twenty years since I'd seen him last – angrily pacing a stage in Philadelphia, arguing that Christians should take back the art world, take back the culture, fight for life. His hair was graying around the angular, serious face I remembered. We sat in a hotel bar and he talked about L'Abri, and about the whole hippie Christian thing. He said evangelicals – like my family – had thought his family was cool because we were 'stupid,' because fundamentalist Christianity was such a limited way of thinking that we were desperate for the Schaeffers' boho intellectual credibility. Then he told me that he was the one who convinced his father to tell Jerry Falwell and James Dobson to put abortion at the top of the evangelical Christian agenda. I asked him about the films – the babies on the assembly line, the dolls scattered on salt flats, the images that convinced me that abortion meant the end of the world. He looked me in the eyes and said, 'Yeah, that was me. That was all me.'

I said, 'It was like a natural disaster was happening.' 'Yeah,' he said. 'We were terrified.' 'Yeah. And I was the one who put those terrifying images in your head.' At this point I had to hold my head, and Frank was quiet for a minute, watching me. It was a kind of earthquake of the synapses, like my brain was rearranging itself. This was only one man, and of course it wasn't all him, but it was him, too, and it had been, it turned out, only a movie. I asked him why he did it. He said that when *Roe v. Wade* happened, he was young, and he had just gotten his girlfriend pregnant, and he thought all babies were his baby, he saw her in every fetus. He wanted us to save her.*

Frank Schaeffer and his father may have been wrong that abortion-on-demand was a slippery slope to state-run infanticide and euthanasia, but something about his images still strikes me as prescient. In the documentary *Food, Inc.*, there are a few seconds of footage of a chicken plant. In row after row of filing

* I'd read later in Schaeffer's book *Crazy for God* that the film series were produced by Gospel Films, on whose board sat the same wealthy Michigan executives, Richard DeVos Sr. and Edgar Prince, who paid for my trip to Washington to march for life. They saw the Schaeffer's films as an opportunity to consolidate the Christian Right, and they couldn't have been more correct.

cabinets, eggs are incubated in metal drawers. After they hatch, a worker shoves the baby chicks through a metal chute onto a conveyor belt. Another worker grabs chicks off the line to debeak them, so that they will not peck each other to death during their brief adult lives, during which they go insane because the intricate social hierarchy that organizes chicken life is not possible in their tiny cages. To watch these clips of factory chicken production – highly subsidized, barely regulated – is to see the horrific vision of the Schaeffers' antiabortion films realized, albeit with a different set of victims. For what abortion meant, for the Schaeffers and then for all of us, was the failure of secular humanism to protect those whose pain doesn't count because they don't count as 'human.'

After she dies, Ingrid Newkirk wants the meat of her body to be barbecued, her skin to be made into purses, her feet to be made into umbrella stands, her eyes to be sent to watch the EPA, and her ears to be sent to the Canadian Parliament to help them hear the screams of baby seals. This is all in her will; she wants to be produced, packaged, and distributed like the animals.

The judge didn't let Scott Roeder talk about abortion during his trial, and on April 1, 2010, he gave him the 'hard fifty': a life sentence with no chance of parole. As he was led out of the courtroom, Roeder shouted, unsurprisingly, 'The blood of babies is on your hands!' Since he murdered Dr. Tiller, Operation

Rescue has struggled to raise operating funds. But Troy Newman has recovered, it seems, from his abortion fatigue – Nebraska abortion doctor LeRoy Carhart has pledged to take over Tiller's late-term business, and Newman has declared war. Our most wanted domestic terrorist, though, is still Daniel San Diego, and no one knows where he is. The FBI claims he's a skilled sailor, so I like to imagine him floating somewhere in green Caribbean waters, tanning his psychopathic tattoos. Meanwhile, Ingrid Newkirk crouches in cages in Times Square, or has cuts of meat diagrammed onto the naked bodies of actresses, as she did for a recent PETA print ad campaign with the slogan 'All Animals Have the Same Parts,' inspiring Jezebel.com blogger Jenna Sauers to write a scathing post against the inhumanity of 'stripping a woman naked and likening her to an animal' with the title 'Ingrid Newkirk Is the Worst Person in the World!'

They take too seriously, these activists, the kinds of suffering that most of us don't think should count. They empathize their way into bodies that aren't even human bodies. They care about the wrong categories of victims, and so they take turns on the altar of our bipartisan ceremonies of rhetorical sacrifice, ceremonies we despise even as we consume them, in a country where we live, still, in the shadow of the cross.

Elizabeth Gumport

– Female Trouble –

W^{*here Art Belongs*}, the title of Chris Kraus's latest collection of essays (Semiotext(e), 2011),
sounds corrective. As if, instead of in its proper place,
art is elsewhere. It has been mislaid, like a cell phone.
Or perhaps, like a vase, not so much lost as thoughtlessly positioned. Where is art, and who put it there?

Anyone who has read Kraus's earlier work can
guess who she'll bring in for questioning. 'Until recently,' Kraus wrote in her previous essay collection,
2004's *Video Green: Los Angeles Art and the Triumph
of Nothingness*, 'there was absolutely no chance of developing an art career in Los Angeles without attending one of several high-profile MFA studio programs,'
including ones at institutions where Kraus herself has
taught. (Since the late 1990s, she has held teaching positions at a number of schools in California, including
UC San Diego, UC Irvine, and Pasadena's Art Center
College of Design.) The MFA is a 'two-year hazing
process' 'essential to the development of value in the
by-nature elusive parameters of neoconceptual art.
Without it, who would know *which* cibachrome photos of urban signage, *which* videotapes of socks toss-
ing around a dryer, *which* neominimalist monochrome

paintings are negligible, and which are destined to be art?'

Duly initiated in sock videos, artists graduate to a handful of galleries, where their advanced degrees re-assure collectors intending to get their money's worth. The MFA is a quality assurance stamp, certifying that no matter what a piece looks like on the surface, it is guaranteed to be full of art-historical references. Alternative exhibition spaces are 'dead-end ghettos, where no one, least of all ambitious students, from the art world goes.' While curators and professors consider the continuum between MFAs and galleries a 'plus' – 'what makes LA so great,' chirps one gallery owner, 'is that the school program is actually a vital part of the community' – Kraus had her doubts. What 'community' were these people talking about? 'It is bizarre,' she observed, 'that here, in America's second largest city, contemporary art should have come to be so isolated and estranged from the experience of the city as a whole.'

Kraus – who was raised in New Zealand, where she worked as a journalist before moving to Manhattan in 1978, when she was 21 – was made similarly uneasy by local zoning policies. There are, she observes, no stores in LA's residential neighborhoods. A city that accepted isolation so indifferently seemed to her an apt symbol for the art world of the 1990s, when the slick conceptualism of the previous decade acquired a harder sheen: sliding doors reflect the pool, the pool the sliding doors – walls of glass, the city eternally showing itself to itself. Like Los Angeles's galleries, the art inside constituted a closed circle of vacuous self-reference. 'Preemptive emptiness' prevailed: 'the greatest triumph of this art work is . . . the way it references so much, content dancing on the surface like a million heated molecules' – angels on the head of a pin and pixels on a screen – 'until you can't pin it down to any given meaning. As such, it is an embodiment of corporate practice: never put into writing what can be mumbled on the phone.'

In *Where Art Belongs*, Kraus continues her assault on neoconceptualism's anticipatory emptiness (or Obliteration, as Stefan Brüggemann – whose work Kraus discusses in the essay 'Twelve Words, Nine Days' – titled his series of squiggly, abstract neon sculptures, illegible 'scribbles,' exhibited in 2007 beside earlier text works whose words Brüggemann had since obscured with silver paint). But the landscape is never far from her mind. In the same chapter, Kraus describes Baja California's condo-lined Highway 1, where billboards advertising new housing developments all use 'some form of the word "life" in their copy: *Life Elevated, Oceanview Life, Live Your Baja Dream . . .*' Trump Baja's slogan is OWNING HERE IS JUST THE BEGINNING. 'The beginning of what?' wonders Kraus. 'The poetics of marketing: since everything is available, the point is no longer to have things but to use them as stations in eternal flux, leveraging into the infinite.'

The 'poetics of marketing' are publicity Esperanto,

the universal language that everyone speaks, whether they're selling a Brüggemann installation or a time-share in Baja. The critics and gallery assistants and freelancers tasked with producing captions and catalog text become copywriters. Their job is 'to give [art] a language that translates into value.' But Brüggemann's original text installations – black vinyl letters stuck straight to the gallery wall – already resembled their own blurbs, art made in the language of the market.

And yet art has newly been spotted *somewhere else*. 'You Are Invited to Be the Last Tiny Creature,' the first essay in *Where Art Belongs*, begins on 'the arterial edge of Echo Park.' Here, in 'a new-ish low-rise cement structure' approximately '20 yards north' of the 101 freeway, Janet Kim launched the art gallery/collective/music label Tiny Creatures in 2006. When it opened, Tiny Creatures neighbored an ice truck and a vacant lot; 99-cent stores stretched into the distance. 'The American Apparel at the corner of Alvarado and Sunset had yet to be built.'

A few years later, Tiny Creatures had become a sensation, warranting a 2009 photo feature in the *Los Angeles Times*, where it 'looks like a portrait of the new LA: neurosurgeons, fashion designers, visitors from London, curators, musicians, and local artists stand outside with drinks, just a few yards from a spot near the freeway where homeless men still sell oranges.' Unfortunately, this was Tiny Creatures' farewell party: Kim and her friends had been priced out of Echo Park.

When Kraus visited in 2010, the entire office complex was abandoned, except for unit 603, which houses a truck-parcel business serving Guatemala.

The collective efforts of Kim and the others affiliated with Tiny Creatures, most of whom had not attended art school and therefore lacked the credentials and unofficial alliances that granted other artists access to LA's art scene, created an alternative to the 'cluster of fiefdoms ruled by a handful of MFA programs.' Tiny Creatures artists were finally invited to mount shows at galleries dominated by credentialed professionals, marking a small reversal of the trend Kraus had identified in *Video Green*, which was the 'shift that has taken place during the past ten years in how art objects reach the market, how they are defined and how we read them. The professionalization of art production – congruent with specialization in other postcapitalist industries – has meant that the only art that will ever reach the market is now art that is produced by graduates of art schools.'

This is the crux of Kraus's true dissatisfaction with the contemporary art world: as the lives of artists started to look ever more alike – high school, college, MFA – they decreased in value. 'The artist's own biography doesn't matter much at all. What life? The blanker the better. The life experience of the artist, if channeled into the artwork, can only impede art's neocorporate, neoconceptual purpose. It is the biography of the *institution* that we want to read.'

And so although 'You Are Invited to Be the Last Tiny Creature' has something of a happy ending – 'when I send [Kim] a draft of this story, she tells me she's just accepted an invitation to curate a new Tiny Creatures show later this year' – it's hard to read it as a success story, or even the whole story. Running contrary to Kraus's enthusiastic assessment of the collective and her analysis of the career trajectories of its artists is the work Tiny Creatures actually produced: Holy Shit frontman Matt Fishbeck's hallucinatory photo collages, Jason Yates's psychedelic posters – a glimpse of this work lets you understand how the Los Angeles art world quickly found a place for it. Tiny Creatures' communal, do-it-yourself ethos might not have aligned exactly with the polished anonymity favored by the art world elite, but that hardly made it antiestablishment.

'Tiny Creatures,' reads the manifesto Kim asked her artists to sign, 'glorifies expression and communication, not the ego.' But if that's the case, then there is nothing assertive or threatening behind such work, no matter where it comes from – nothing that might mean its interest in and presentation of personal experience would pose a danger to, or be radically or even slightly different from, that of a branded artist like Brüggemann, where the ego is contained in familiar credentials and the fatuous cant of the artist's statement. The 'artist's statement'! So like the college applicant's personal statement, where the teenage supplicant appeals to institutions by formalizing confessed, 'unique' experiences, in the same moralistic language used by every other high school student in America.

The real threats are artists who refuse to stop there – who move from confession, which describes a situation, to analysis, which seeks to explain it. If someone foolishly insists on making his – or her – life known, institutions have words for discrediting it. *This candidate can't be admitted.* As Kraus declared in *Video Green*:

I think that 'privacy' is to contemporary female art what 'obscenity' was to male art and literature of the 1960s. The willingness of someone to use her life as primary material is still deeply disturbing, and even more so if she views her own experience at some remove. There is no problem with female confession providing it is made within a repentant therapeutic narrative. But to examine things coolly, to thrust experience out of one's own brain and put it on the table, is still too confrontational.

If the sufferer describes a pathology that is socially approved, because privately felt, personally inflicted, and guiltily accepted as such (anorexia, addiction, sexual misadventures of all varieties), great. If it is socially determined and experienced by a person who knows she is sane and lucid and doesn't want to get well – who will not even identify as sick – well, that's not so cool. If it's not her problem, then whose is it?

'Why do people still not get it when we handle vulnerability like philosophy, at some remove?' Kraus wonders in her first novel, 1997's *I Love Dick*, which – like her other novels, *Aliens and Anorexia* (2000) and

Torpor (2006) – is an attempt to do exactly that. (All three are mixtures of criticism, autobiography, and fiction that explicitly include and describe Kraus's efforts to convert her biography into fiction.) Female artists who refuse to enter 'the realm of abject memoir/confession' and insist on talking about their private experiences – about sex, pain, drugs, and the ordinary, universal nuisance of living inside a body – will be called 'immoral' anyway.

In *Video Green*, Kraus cited the case of Jennifer Schlosberg, who was a 26-year-old art student at UCLA when she produced *78 Drawings of My Face*, 'an alphabetized dossier' of 'the history of her interactions with everyone at school.' Everyone at school? Not anonymous sexual partners? Not even generic art world archetypes? Students and faculty members were furious. Professors refused to work with her. 'Why do you make yourself so scary?' asked Schlosberg's adviser, the conceptual artist Chris Burden, the same man who made his career by filming himself being shot with a gun and nailed, in front of a crowd, to a Volkswagen. 'Artists,' Burden explained to his young student, 'have to do their own work. Art should not be based on social interactions.'

Schlosberg's nearly accidental stumbling into reality, and social reality, as the unnameable thing – as fundamentally scandalous – cuts to the heart of Kraus's quarrel with MFA programs. When Kraus offered an elective on diary writing at an art school in California, the students who signed up were 'mostly girls, of course, who'd drifted foolishly into art, thinking art might be a medium for change or self-expression. . . . Unlike the girls who'd go on to good careers making videotapes of lawn-sprinklers, the diary-writers wondered why there were no senior female faculty at the school and why the Institution's only black employees were security guards and secretaries. The diary-writers wondered why the institution's only class on "feminism" was perennially taught by men.' Looking around the curriculum, Kraus noticed that the 'confrontational, conceptual female artists who were Burden's prominent contemporaries' had been corralled into single-semester electives or pushed off syllabi entirely.

Kraus associates the disappearance of most of these women artists – from reading lists and libraries, from our chronology of the end of the 20th century, with the erasure of radical feminist intellectuals like Shulamith Firestone, author of *The Dialectic of Sex*. (Firestone, writing about her hopes for artists in 1970: 'Within the next decade, we may see [female art's] growth into a powerful new art . . . that will, for the first time, authentically grapple with the reality that women live in.') Out of print for many years, *Dialectic* was reissued by FSG in 2003, thanks to the efforts of the younger feminist Jennifer Baumgardner. Now it's out of print again. 'As a teenager,' Kraus writes, '*Dialectic* was my favorite book, and I'd always wondered what had happened to Shulamith.'

What had happened is that, after years of trying to tell the world the truth, she spent over a decade 'shuttling in and out of New York City public mental hospitals,' an experience she finally documented in 1998's *Airless Spaces*, a series of 'very short and barely fictionalized observations.' Like *Where Art Belongs*, it was published by Semiotext(e), where Kraus has been an editor for over two decades.

At Semiotext(e), Kraus shares editorial duties with Hedi El Kholti and her ex-husband and Semiotext(e) founding father Sylvère Lotringer. Born in France to Polish Jews who fled Warsaw in 1930, Lotringer spent much of his childhood in hiding outside Paris. After the war, he moved to Israel with his family, then returned to France, spending several years as a member of the Socialist-Zionist youth movement Hashomer Hatzair before entering the Sorbonne in 1958. He completed his graduate work at the École Pratique des Hautes Études, where he wrote an unusual dissertation on Virginia Woolf under the supervision of Roland Barthes. Columbia University hired Lotringer as a professor in the early 1970s – as he dates it, 'just a few months after the publication of *Anti-Oedipus*' – and, in New York, he quickly established the journal *Semiotext(e)* 'as a bridge' by which the work of Deleuze and Guattari and other exemplars of the newest French theory might be imported to America.

Despite a nominal university affiliation, *Semiotext(e)*

was subsidized largely by Lotringer and his staff, which included Kathryn Bigelow – the *Hurt Locker* director got her start directing a twenty-minute short featuring two men punching each other, while Lotringer and Marshall Blonsky analyzed the action in voice-over. They had published several issues when they began organizing an ambitious 'Schizo-Culture' conference on prisons and madness. Guattari persuaded Deleuze to accompany him to New York. Foucault, who was teaching in Brazil, agreed to stop by on his way back to Paris. (At work on *The History of Sexuality*, he was enticed by the prospect of examining a rare Jesuit education manual held by the New York Public Library.) In 1975, the 2,000 attendees who descended upon Columbia's campus witnessed what Foucault called 'the last counterculture event of the '60s.' Lotringer recalls:

As for Deleuze, he managed to present an outline of his concept of the 'rhizome,' which had not yet been discussed in print – but in French, very slowly, while drawing diagrams of root systems and crabgrass on a blackboard. Foucault, who was already known in America, looked on while his paper on infantile sexuality, an attack on radical academics who mistook their verbal pronouncements against repression for political action, was read aloud by a friend in English. When the lecture was over, members of Lyndon LaRouche's Labor Committee instantly created havoc by denouncing Foucault (and [R. D.] Laing) as undercover CIA agents. In this climate, Semiotext(e) came into being as a cultural venture, and not just a semiotic outfit.

And Semiotext(e) permanently transformed the landscape of American thought. Both the magazine and the books series, which Lotringer established in 1983, played 'a pathbreaking role in the early diffusion of French theory,' François Cusset writes in *French Theory: How Foucault, Derrida, Deleuze, & Co. Transformed the Intellectual Life of the United States*. The small, black, inexpensive paperbacks published by Semiotext(e)'s Foreign Agents imprint introduced a generation of American students to a number of French authors, among them Paul Virilio, Jean-François Lyotard, and Jean Baudrillard. (The first title in the series – an excerpt adapted from Baudrillard's *Simulacra and Simulation* – sold more than 20,000 copies.) Lotringer imagined these complex but unacademic volumes as how-to books: what they taught you was 'how to think with your own mind . . . how to eroticize thinking, make it a pleasure of the senses.' It was, he declared, 'philosophy for the boudoir.'

Lotringer has famously called French theory an 'American invention.' At the least, it was a collaborative effort. French *soixante-huitard* theorists, prone to futurism, prediction, and occasional grandiose exaggeration, wound up telling the truth about what it felt like to live in hypercapitalist, postindustrial America, which embodied – and responded to – their ideas with more enthusiasm than France ever would. To American literary people (and university literature departments), theory felt vital in a way that novels no longer did. It was the inheritor of modernism's 'many-sided ambitiousness,' as Terry Eagleton put it – a certain capacious, cosmopolitan dissidence, a restless spirit that could not be satisfied or expressed in any of the old ways.

Meanwhile, another void was waiting to be filled – in the art world, where neo-expressionism was on the way out. The launch of the Foreign Agents series in 1983 corresponded with the rise of neoconceptualism, whose advocates and practitioners championed self-reflexive art, work that absorbed consumer society in order to critique it. Barthes, whose *Mythologies* everyone had read in art school, was a major early influence, but it was Baudrillard – visionary theorist of the consumer society – who became their hero. *Artforum* put him on its masthead. (Nobody checked with Baudrillard, who was surprised to see himself listed as a contributing editor.) When the Whitney invited Baudrillard to give 'A Distinguished Lecture on American Art and Culture of the Twentieth Century' in 1987, a competing Anti-Baudrillard show was organized downtown. Lotringer arranged a third event: a lecture at Columbia University, where Baudrillard announced that many of his avowed followers had misunderstood his work entirely.

The art scene's 'deadly embrace' of Baudrillard confirmed Lotringer's suspicion that French theory had become 'dangerously popular.' Intended in part as a symbolic burial of theory – in the very place it was born – the 1987 Columbia lecture was also an acknowledgment of the fact it had taken on a zombie afterlife of its own. So, as armies of the undead continued to buy its backlist, the question pressed: besides serve as the executor of its own estate, what would Semiotext(e) do? Who would recall it to life?

Kraus – who had met Lotringer earlier that decade, when she was working to make a name for herself as an artist and filmmaker in the downtown circles in which he was revered – suggested Semiotext(e) turn to face America directly and recover the original, unpardonably forgotten contribution the United States had made to intellectual life in the years after 1968, namely, feminism. This recovery took the form of the Native Agents series. When the imprint was launched in 1990, with Kraus as editor, Foreign Agents had never published a book by someone who wasn't a white man. Semiotext(e) had 'missed out' on the feminist movement entirely. 'It happened,' Lotringer told an interviewer, 'and I wasn't aware of it.' He hadn't published women, Kraus explained, 'because the only women he knew writing theory were doing psychoanalytic theory, which he wasn't so interested in.'

Native Agents sought to recover a different line of feminism, publishing female authors who used what Kraus described as 'the same public "I" that gets expressed in these other French theories . . . a personal "I" that is constantly bouncing up against the world – that isn't just existing for itself.' Its first titles were Ann Rower's *If You're a Girl and Walking Through Clear*

Water in a Pool Painted Black by the actress and down-town activist Cookie Mueller. Mueller had inspired the title of John Waters's 1974 'bad taste' masterpiece *Female Trouble*. When Mueller was hospitalized with pelvic inflammatory disease, Waters visited and asked her what was wrong. 'Just a little female trouble, hon,' she quipped. Neither Mueller nor Rower shied away from the taboos of the female body in their writing, which addressed the mysterious, atmospheric shyness when it came to women's lives. 'It seems weird how all these embarrassing female type stories seemed to be popping into my mind, and then into my writing,' Rower explains in the very first paragraph of *If You're a Girl*. '[S]tories about sex, abuse, rape, abortion, marriage, divorce, infection, kids. I want to make a collection of them and call it *If You're a Girl*.' A few other titles were proposed; people took offense to all of them. 'Touchy subject,' Rower admits. 'But then all the interesting subjects were touchy. Or taken.'

What united the Native Agents authors was the way their work combined elements of theory, fiction, and biography, explicitly refusing to identify absolutely with any single genre. The last lines of *If You're a Girl* could have served as Native Agents' call to arms: 'Can I help it,' Rower wrote, 'if I wanna put back the lie in Li(t)erature, as in Li(f)e? Go ahead, Plato, make my day.' It was a challenge that other Native Agents writers like the novelist Lynne Tillman, and Eileen Myles – whose poetry small presses had been publishing since the late 1970s – had been issuing for some time. Tillman started writing 'critical fiction' in the early 1980s, when she was asked to produce a piece to accompany an exhibition of Kiki Smith's drawings. What she came up with was a first-person account narrated by the sort-of-fictional, sort-of-art-critic Madame Realism, who watches TV, goes to dinner parties, and muses on Dalí. In the final paragraph of 'Madame Realism,' Madame Realism looks at herself in the mirror, pets her cat, turns off the TV. A story, she decides, is 'a way to think.'

Because of Semiotext(e)'s cachet, Native Agents offered these authors a chance their work might find – and be taken seriously by – a wider audience. In 1992, Semiotext(e) brought out *The Madame Realism Complex*, a collection of Tillman's critical fiction, or fictional criticism, including the original 'Madame Realism.' Amplified, Tillman's voice – and Myles's (her 1991 collection *Not Me* was Native Agents' third book), and Firestone's in *Airless Spaces* – reached new ears. Their style and method influenced younger Semiotext(e) authors, including Michelle Tea (*The Passionate Mistakes and Intricate Corruption of One Girl in America*, 1998) and Veronica Gonzalez (*twin time: or, how death befell me*, 2007).

As it turned out, the most gifted practitioner of Native Agents' nonpsychoanalytic first-person mode proved to be Kraus herself. 'To be female still means being trapped within the purely psychological. . . . Because emotion's just so terrifying the world refuses to believe that it can be pursued as discipline, as form. . . . *If women have failed to make "universal" art because we're trapped within the "personal," why not universalize the "personal" and make it the subject of our art?'* she wondered in *I Love Dick*, in which she aimed to do exactly that.

The novel begins with 'Chris Kraus' falling suddenly and electrically in love with 'Dick [Hebdige],' an English cultural critic and friend of her husband 'Sylvère Lotringer.' Like Kraus and Lotringer, 'Chris' and 'Sylvère' met on the New York art scene of the 1980s, where he was an established figure and she an aspiring director. Over the years, 'Sylvère's' star seems to burn increasingly bright, while her projects fail to find funding or an audience. Like her, they simply are not taken seriously: 'Because she does not express herself in theoretical language, no one' – meaning none of Sylvère's friends in the upper echelons of the art world or academia – 'expects too much from her.' With Dick, things go similarly. They have sex, then he rebuffs her advances and dismisses her writing – first the letters she sends him about their encounters and her subsequent fantasies, then the stories she writes about sending those letters, and finally the ones about *publishing* those letters and stories.

'If I could *love you consciously*,' she declares, 'take an experience that was so completely female and subject it to an abstract analytical system, then perhaps I had a chance of understanding something and could go on living.' Exegesis begins in eros; interpretation is not simply a method but an instructive technique. 'Love is like writing,' reflects Kraus, and, immune to boredom, the lover is the ideal critic, her attention happily and effortlessly held. Meaning shines from the most mundane details, which Kraus connects into constellations of particular and luminous significance. It is possible, she finds, to turn on in ourselves the bright light of the interrogation room – to willfully and willingly aim our minds at ourselves; to expose all experience always to direct and sustained evaluation. Through the intentional, perpetual effort to comprehend it, existence is transformed from a series of events lived through into a whole and single life – and therefore the world in which it is lived into something within our power to comprehend. As long as we question our authority to evaluate the universe, the universe remains a question not only open but inscrutable. What is known to us tells us what there is to know: what it has the answer for – and all that it has to answer for.

I Love Dick ends with a FedEx package sent by Hebdige to the address 'Sylvère' and 'Chris' share: inside are two envelopes, one for Sylvère, the other for Chris, who has been waiting to hear from him. She opens the one for Sylvère first: 'I should have,' Dick has written, 'been absolutely unambiguous in my response to the letters you and Kris [surely a contender for the most perverse *sic* in the history of *sics*!] sent over the following month instead of opting for bemused silence. . . . I still enjoy your company and conversation when we meet and believe, as you do, that Kris has talent as a writer. . . . I do not share your conviction that my right to privacy has to be sacrificed for the sake of that talent.' Then she opens the envelope addressed to her – and finds a photocopy of the same letter. The gesture is a masterstroke of indifference. More than a personal rejection, it is a dismissal of Chris *as a person*, as an individual worthy of engaging in conversation, or even correctly identifying.

Shortly after *I Love Dick* was released, *New York* magazine reported that Hebdige had attempted to block publication of the book on grounds that it invaded his privacy. 'I don't like reading bad reviews,' he said, 'and this book reads like a bad review of my presence in the world. . . . If someone's writing gets read because it exploits a recognizable figure, then it really is a despicable exercise.' Kraus defended her project on the grounds it 'explod[ed] the "right of privacy" that serves patriarchy so well.' Hebdige scoffed: 'A feminist issue? Tell her to take it up with Princess Diana.'

It's hard not to feel sympathy for Hebdige, author of the classic *Subculture: The Meaning of Style*, who – in the pre-Twitter, pre-Facebook twilight of the 20th century – understandably assumed intimate facts about his existence would never be made public. Even today, we generally trust we will be the ones in control of the broadcast. Wouldn't we behave differently if we really, truly believed we weren't? Our lives, not quite ours, would go in part unlived.

But privacy *is* a feminist issue, one that underlies so many others. As the labor movement made questions of 'private' property and private time into public issues, women's liberation swung open the door of the home to reveal the political dimensions of childcare and domestic labor. It was a door that had long been locked: domestic work was not really uncompensated labor, the assumption went, because love paid the wages. The natural affection a mother felt for her child set parenting apart from other kinds of activity. A similar logic ran through 19th-century America's arguments against giving women the vote, or property rights: all men, first as sons and then as husbands, were privately influenced by women. By exerting this influence, women were as good as represented. Private relationships constituted, or compensated for, public recognition. Women held the key to no kingdom: they belonged outside the public sphere, and yet were denied a private life of their own.

Historically, privacy has not defended the autonomy of women, but perpetuated the lie that they are *already* free. It becomes clear that even what sounds like a positive guarantee of privacy actually denies it to women if one listens closely to the words of one of the most famous defenses of a woman's right to privacy, *Roe v. Wade*. Writing for the majority, Harry Blackmun declared that 'the right of privacy, however based, is broad enough to cover [a woman's decision to have an abortion]; that the right, nonetheless, is not absolute and is subject to some limitations; and that at some point the state interests as to protection of health, medical standards, and prenatal life, become dominant. . . . The woman's right to privacy is no longer sole and any right of privacy she possesses must be measured accordingly.' Until then, abortion was to be considered 'a medical decision,' responsibility for which 'must rest with the physician.' In his concurrence with the majority opinion, William O. Douglas specified that the privacy protected by the ruling was *not* a woman's, but 'that between physician and patient.' A woman's right to privacy, in other words, was contingent; at a certain point in time, it would cease to exist. Until then, it resided in her relationship with her doctor.

What the pretense of privacy often does is protect us from reality. It is called on to conceal the fact that there are *two* realities: the world as it is lived in by men, and the world of women, which has historically been exiled from political and philosophical consideration. It has been regarded as *beneath* such consideration, its truths narrowly and inescapably personal – rather than universal – and therefore inevitably trivial. Hence Hebdige's invocation of Princess Diana: a woman's life, presented in public, was always the stuff of tabloids. She should be glad not to have it exhibited, and ashamed to exhibit it herself. ('Why,' wonders Kraus in *I Love Dick*, 'does everybody think that women are debasing themselves when we expose the conditions of our debasement?') Placing domestic and intimate relationships outside the boundaries of legitimate public interest in this way condemns them permanently to the status of intractable nature, or 'frivolous gossip,' discouraging intervention and thereby preserving invisible practices of domination. After all, only social problems have social solutions. It is no coincidence that feminism's furthest advances have been made in spaces already considered public (offices, voting booths), while the demands it places on 'the private sphere' (like those concerning the division of household labor and childcare) face enduring resistance.

If privacy is defined in such a way that it handicaps the ability of certain people to enter freely and equally into public life, it is not only a meaningless concept but a despicable one. When Kraus exploded privacy, what she demolished was a house beyond repair – sweeping away 'privacy' in its present contradictory state so something that could be enjoyed, for the first time, equally and freely by both men and women, might take its place.

As Kraus writes in *I Love Dick*:

Because most 'serious' fiction, still, involves the fullest possible expression of a single person's subjectivity, it's considered crass and amateurish not to 'fictionalize' the supporting cast of characters, changing names and insignificant features of their identities. The 'serious contemporary hetero-male novel' is a thinly veiled Story of Me, as voraciously consumptive as all of patriarchy. While the hero/anti-hero explicitly is the author, everybody else is reduced to 'characters.' . . .

When women try to pierce this false conceit by naming names because our 'I's are changing as we meet other 'I's, we're called bitches, libelers, pornographers, and amateurs.

Bitches, libelers, whatever word you want to use: the point is they are *naming names*: mapping out their individual consciousness means recognizing the other individuals that shaped its borders, and acknowledging them as such. The purpose of such personal details is to represent a shared reality – to capture the familiar feeling of never feeling like yourself, but a series of selves, whether past, present, potential, or imagined by others – but also perhaps to change it. This, Kraus explains in the essay 'May '69' in *Where Art Belongs*, was the utopian intent of the liberation movements of the late 1960s and '70s and in particular the British sex magazine *Suck*, whose 'editors routinely invaded their own and each other's privacy,' appearing nude in the paper and writing openly about their sexual experiences. 'Sexuality and daily life were seen as the locus of politics'; the public exposure of traditionally private behavior 'a means of disrupting the social order.' Who today believes 'it might be possible to live differently,' or even wants to?

In the end, Kraus agreed to cut Hebdige's last name and other identifying details from the final draft, and *I Love Dick* was published.

Over the years, *I Love Dick* has become a cult classic, as have books by other Native Agents authors, including Bernadette Corporation's *Reena Spaulings* and Eileen Myles's *Not Me*. Like Kraus, Myles is well-respected and devoutly admired, as are many of the series's writers, Howe, Tillman, and Kathy Acker among them. (*Where Art Belongs* is the first of Kraus's books to be published by a different Semiotext(e) brand: the Intervention Series, established in 2009, publishes 'polemical texts,' whose authors – Kraus so far has been the only exception to this rule – are men or, potentially, unnamed or anonymous female members of Tiqqun and the Invisible Committee.) Yet Native Agents has never attained the incendiary authority wielded by Semiotext(e)'s other, earlier branches. After Semiotext(e) cut ties with the publishing collective Autonomedia in 2000, it found a new distributor in MIT Press, which was enticed by the strength of Semiotext(e)'s backlist of French authors and Lotringer's professional contacts. Then editor-in-chief Larry Cohen had to be talked into taking on the fiction.

In the years since, Kraus's – and Native Agents' – star has grown brighter. Yet both remain on the periphery of academia, which so warmly embraced the first generation of Semiotext(e) authors. François Cusset, who in *French Theory* spends many pages rightly and lucidly praising the work of Semiotext(e) and Lotringer, dispenses with Native Agents in a single, subordinate clause, describing its titles as 'political autofictions and collections of lesbian short stories.' Kraus is identified as Lotringer's 'companion.'

Cusset's account of the Schizo-Culture conference in 1975 is similarly unsatisfying: 'Deleuze, for whom this was the one and only trip across the Atlantic, was interrupted in his debate with Ronald Laing by a far Left militant feminist, Ti-Grace Atkinson, who worked her way to the front and began to insult them, calling them 'phallocrats' and preventing them from continuing.' If only Deleuze's American vacation hadn't been ruined by that crazy woman! You wouldn't know from Cusset's account that Atkinson had actually been invited to participate in the conference. (And surely Atkinson deserves at least to be *the* 'far Left militant feminist,' on the basis of her extensive, ambitious, and pivotal historical role in US radical feminism, of which it is still professionally acceptable for historians to be blithely unaware.) Instead, the wording accuses her of those particularly feminine crimes, shrillness and irrationality. *What is this woman talking about? Why can't she just shut up?*

Other reports have cast Atkinson's behavior at the conference in a somewhat less fearsome light. In one possible past, a crowd of supporters boos Guattari off the stage for allowing a band to set up behind him just before Atkinson is scheduled to speak. What a twist! It's like finding out that Arthur Conan Doyle wrote a version of 'A Scandal in Bohemia' in which Irene Adler steals a photograph from Sherlock Holmes. The story is the same, but the characters have switched places. The man we thought was Deleuze is actually his double, Guattari, and the crime he's charged with – preventing someone else from speaking – is exactly the one Atkinson is accused of.

When *I Love Dick* was reprinted in 2006, Eileen Myles contributed a new introduction in which she characterized Kraus's fusion of fiction, autobiography, and criticism as a successful turning of the tables. 'Not on a particular guy, "Dick," but on that smug impervious observing culture' – 'the male host culture,' which she forces 'to listen to her describe the *inside* of those famous female feelings.' The *inside*: like the inside of the desk drawer, where one's unsent letters are kept, or the inside of the envelope, which holds the unread letter.

And the letter – in some cases, the fax – is the foundation of *I Love Dick*: first with Sylvère, then on her own, Chris writes hundreds of letters to Dick documenting and analyzing her feelings for him. And she writes them in full knowledge of the fact that letter-writing has long been considered a female occupation. By the 1870s, the stereotype had congealed firmly enough that Flaubert could satirize 'epistolary style' as 'reserved exclusively for women' in his *Dictionary of*

Received Ideas. For well over a century, women had been rigorously trained in the art of writing letters while being praised for their 'natural' letter-writing abilities: it was, declared one Frenchman in 1665, 'an art that they have learned without thinking about it.' The invention of what Katharine Ann Jensen calls the 'Epistolary Woman' effectively excluded all women from the sphere of serious male conversation. Although women played a crucial role in the Republic of Letters and the development of Romantic philosophy – think, for instance, of such female *salonnières* as Germaine de Staël, whose writing introduced France to German philosophy and Romanticism's exaltation of enthusiasm as the emotion on which knowledge and happiness most depended – they found that the boundaries of that Republic were ultimately drawn such that their letters were excluded.

Rousseau's *Julie*, Richardson's *Pamela* and *Clarissa*, even naughty *Fanny Hill*: the earliest novels consisted of letters from women, writing always and only about love. But men, of course, were the ones writing these novels. If, as critics have suggested, the epistolary novel was the crucible of modern consciousness – of third-person narration in fiction ('the person most girls use when they want to talk about themselves but don't think anyone will listen,' reflects Kraus in *I Love Dick* – after, it's worth noting, she's switched over to the first person), of our every and own thoughts in life – the female mind it molded was built to hold thoughts of love. 'Eventually,' writes Kraus, Chris and Sylvère 'would title [one section of their correspondence] *Does the Epistolary Genre Mark the Advent of the Bourgeois Novel?* But that was later, after another dinner with some noted academic friends at Dick's,' when a 'poised and glamorous' curator calls Chris's project 'so bourgeois' and cites Habermas. (That would be the Habermas of *The Structural Transformation of the Public Sphere*, which he will attribute not to salons – steered and attended by women, located inside private homes – but to newspaper reading in coffeehouses, where women were not welcome.) Chris, silent, barely touches her food.

Like *I Love Dick*, Kraus's semiautobiographical novel *Torpor* is narrated by someone who is perceived by many of the people she encounters to play a nonspeaking role. Set in the early 1990s, Torpor tells the story of Sylvie – an aspiring filmmaker – and her partner Jerome – a French academic – who, with the (ultimately unfulfilled) goal of adopting a Romanian orphan, embark together on a doomed voyage across Eastern Europe. The journey includes a stop in Berlin, where Jerome has a summer fellowship. When two German poets putting together an anthology of American countercultural writing ask Jerome to serve as their third coeditor, Sylvie insists on attending the meeting. This is, after all, her area of expertise: like Kraus, Sylvie edits 'a fiction series for Jerome's press'; like Native Agents, its authors are mostly women who do not so much let the reader in as announce themselves as 'a female public I aimed outwards towards the world.'

At the meeting, while discussing possible contributors, 'the three men reel off the names of other men. All white. Sylvie finds the reality of this unbearable. Finally she says: "You know, there aren't any women on this list." . . . She's been around this world for 15 years and knows that there are never any women on the list, unless someone consciously decides to put them there.' She suggests a few but 'no one in the room has heard of any of these writers. . . . The men just gape as Sylvie mounts a passionate defense of how *female lived experience can be channeled through poetic avant-gardist forms, but in the process changes them.*'

Why, she demands afterward, didn't Jerome – who knows little about the kind of writing that's to be included in the anthology – just tell the Germans she should be their collaborator, since in all likelihood she'll end up doing most of the work? It's his name they're paying for, he tells her, and he's right. Sylvie may share a 'wealth of philosophic-literary references' with Jerome – and, in effect, a transposition of the real Sylvère's name – but 'in terms of *opportunities*,' she's poorer than him. Why don't their investments pay off the same?

For so long, so many lives refused to be lived like books! Because the books, in turn, were not truly like lives. One way in which they failed to account for female experience was by not acknowledging that failure to account for female experience – that constant feeling of being told, *you are telling your life the wrong way*. You are taking your life personally, which is to say: not like an artist. In *I Love Dick*, Kraus quotes a letter Flaubert wrote to Louise Colet, after he read *La Servante*, a poem about a young woman who, like Colet, loves books and a writer who scorns her: 'You have made Art an outlet for the passions, a kind of chamberpot to catch the overflow of I don't know what. It doesn't smell good! It smells of hate!' Her poem was not so much a bad poem as a bad review of his life, to use Hebdige's phrase. Colet's description of universal experience had not thoroughly enough been scraped of her *personal* experience and was therefore not universal.

But what was the universal? At what point did an account of human experience spill over into the trivial? Female experience constituted art up until the point it ceased to be identical with male experience. (Flaubert to Colet: 'You are a poet shackled to a woman!') And so to live one's life as a woman was at odds with living one's life as if it were a work of art – not just because certain elements particular to female existence tended not to make their way into most novels but because most novels, if they were good, refused to acknowledge that the world maintained such crucial distinctions. There should always and only be the human – and we all wanted to be human.

Kraus's decision to 'explode privacy' is nothing

less than an attempt to make books equal to life, so that we may have books to live by. If theory filled a void left by the novel, work like Kraus's takes up where both left off. The truth about life must be told, in one form or another, and Kraus offers another way of telling. Flaubert, quoted by Kraus in her introduction to the Barnes & Noble edition of *Madame Bovary*, writes: 'Work is still the best means of getting the better of life' – and so lives must be allowed to count as work before they can be gotten the better of.

Could it be, then, that what Kraus is at work on is a kind of philosophy, philosophy that simply goes unrecognized as such? (It's happened before. Terry Eagleton suggests one reason American philosophy departments failed to embrace French theory was that it simply did not sound like philosophy.) As Kraus knew it would be, which is perhaps the point, or part of it: 'What hooks me on our story,' Kraus tells Dick, 'is our different readings of it. You think it's personal and private; my neurosis. . . . I think our story is performative philosophy.' She has another name for it, too: 'American first-person fiction.' And that insistence on the first-person, that ever-developing 'I': who does Kraus sound like here so much as Thoreau? Thoreau, with his famous ironic and then sincere statement, early in *Walden*: 'In most books, the I, or first person, is omitted; in this it will be retained; that, in respect to egotism, is the main difference. We commonly do not remember that it is, after all, always the first person that is speaking.

I should not talk so much about myself if there were anybody else whom I knew as well. Unfortunately, I am confined to this theme by the narrowness of my experience. Moreover, I, on my side, require of every writer, first or last, a simple and sincere account of his own life, and not merely what he has heard of other men's lives; some such account as he would send to his kindred from a distant land; for if he has lived sincerely, it must have been in a distant land to me.'

'IS THE UNREPRESENTED LIFE WORTH LIVING?' wonders Lynn Tillman's Madame Realism. 'NO TAXATION WITHOUT REPRESENTATION.' Yes, the whole country has always had female trouble! And it ails us still. *Torpor* begins with a quotation that describes how to identify sugar maples, taken from the 1936 edition of Clarence Moores Weed's field guide *Our Trees, How to Know Them*. ('The following pages,' Weed touchingly explains in his introduction, 'are intended to furnish an opportunity for a more intimate acquaintance with our American trees.') Life – here, now, on this continent, in all its prosaic particularity – is something that can be known, is something we might reasonably be said to have knowledge of. There is nothing in the world without a name, or to which we might not give one, should we deem it worthy. What Thoreau, for instance, found worthy was his own life, as lived by him, in America. As a writer, editor, and publisher, Kraus takes up this native tradition, which historically has been best obeyed by those who defied it

– by those who understood its meaning, and so sought to redefine it. Both her writing and the Native Agents series as a whole attempt nothing more or less than to cure us of our female trouble by making Thoreau's treatment available to women, to whom it has so often been denied. To let, in other words, women treat themselves as worth treating, as Kraus does in *I Love Dick*: 'She was an American artist, and for the first time it occurred to her that perhaps the only thing she had to offer was her specificity. By writing *Dick* she was offering her life as a Case Study.'

Nikil Saval

– A Labor Movement –

Among the endless, nearly bureaucratic proliferation of working groups at Occupy Wall Street and elsewhere – people of color, sanitation, media, alternative banking, sustainability, anti-racism allies, disability – one stands out for its simultaneous universality and total narrowness. The labor working group, in any occupation, has a very clear and dully unobjectionable task: to help get material support from trade unions for the protests. Usually it consists of people who are union members, who have real but limited ways of getting in touch with their union leadership to encourage them to endorse the various occupations. In this modest task, the labor working groups have been successful: most trade unions, as well as the largest national labor federation, have serviced the occupations in ways that have helped them sustain themselves over the long haul.

But 'labor' means – or should mean – much more than the parlous remainder of American trade unionism. It means 'work,' and it means 'jobs.' From Locke, we retain the notion that labor is the source of property, what you put your hands into; from Smith, Ricardo, and Marx, that it is the source of the value of commodities.

Labor is the thing one does to sustain life, and thing that one hates for that very reason; it creates wealth, and it takes wealth away from the wealthiest. Everything we make for our wants and want to make is labor.

In the more material sense, campaigns for higher wages, employment, sounder trade policies, and a fairer economy have always come from the traditional labor movement. Yet it fell not to labor but the short-lived and controversial demands working group to argue that Occupy Wall Street should number full employment among its chief demands. The renegade methods of the group garnered more discussion than the fact that a (parsimonious) full employment bill already passed as legislation in the 1970s – the Humphrey-Hawkins Full Employment Act – whose impetus and traces of radicalism (mostly expunged by the Chamber of Commerce, which helped to water down the bill) come from the American labor movement, which pushed the hardest for its victory.

I mean to say that the occupations are in danger of treating labor the same way the Democratic Party treats it: as a source of bodies and money, a mere service that tends to be thanked and repudiated in the same breath. Labor, in this way, is like the homeless: it lends legitimacy to but also threatens the burgeoning movement. In a recent *New York Times* article, one protester is quoted as saying, 'We're glad to have unions endorse us, but we can't formally endorse them. We're an autonomous group and it's important to keep our autonomy.' The protester, like all occupiers, speaks for himself, but for anyone who has heard the discourse on labor coming out of the protests, the comment is emblematic. At a panel hosted by the magazine *Jacobin* in early October, one of the participants, speaking in the cavalier language of Italian autonomism, derided the efficacy of 'union marches.' The message is rather clear: Labor unions are welcome to assist the occupations, but they shouldn't expect any help in return. Of course, despite the usual reservations that people have about labor unions and the relegation of issues that should be central to a single, largely unheralded working group, a substantial handful of occupiers have turned out for actions in support of 'union marches' – at Sotheby's, Verizon, and elsewhere – much as students in the supposedly hostile New Left did. The same *New York Times* article notes that labor unions have been inspired by the occupations to turn to civil disobedience – a tactic that the labor movement pioneered in the face of much worse violence than flash bombs and tear gas, and which they have in fact practiced to this very day. Even the form of the occupation derives in large part, despite or perhaps because of the left's dim memory bank, from the sit-down strike.

In keeping labor unions at a safe distance, the occupations are also in danger of evacuating the concept they have done the most to revive: 'solidarity.' At a recent *n+1* panel on Occupy Wall Street, the term came up in a discussion of unions that supported the XL

Keystone Pipeline (construction unions, predictably). One panelist argued that we could have 'solidarity' with certain institutions without supporting everything they do. But that form of solidarity is just genial condescension. Solidarity – a term that came out of the nascent French labor movement of the 1840s – isn't the same as coalition building: it entails an entire way of life and being in the world, of cementing ties between equals, not a grudging respect between interest groups. In the case of the pipeline, there are several unions (Transit Workers United, Amalgamated Transit Union, Canada's Communications, Energy and Paperworkers Union) that have come out against it. As for the unions that support it, the task of solidarity is not mourning their failure to be as smart as us, but organizing them to be true to shared ideals. Occupiers and those of us who are fellow-travelers cannot act as if we have no obligation to change labor unions to help their goals – as if the one existing institution that has more or less consistently fought for every economic goal they espouse isn't worth transforming, enlarging, and moving.

It's worth asking ourselves, on the occupying left, how we plan to reduce inequality without increasing wages; foster employment without cementing the protections against unemployment; ensure that the old retire with dignity without protecting pensions. If there is a single force that has successfully fought for these things besides the labor movement, I'd like to see it.

As for their much-despised 'bureaucratic' nature, it's hard to see how the occupations – with their teams of lawyers and their masses of committees – have a higher soapbox to stand on.

Recent polls suggest that a majority of Americans would, if given the chance, join a labor union; the same polls suggest that a majority of Americans have an unfavorable view of labor unions. Americans want to have more control over the way they work, but they don't like the form that control tends to take. They like labor, but they hate Labor. This is precisely the paradox that the occupiers face within their own ranks; it indicates a real hostility to an actual problem but it also suggests that the only way forward is to change that perception. People can endlessly rehearse to themselves the failures of traditional trade unionism, or they can try to change the one available form of organization that promises to deliver the things they want. It has already become customary to speak of the 'Occupy Movement.' But most movements of the past have been clearly for or against something. The antiwar movement. The civil rights movement. The women's liberation movement. The 'Occupy Movement,' which, when it lets its guard down, admits that it wants equality, might do worse than submitting to a name that represents the struggle for it in the past, and call itself a 'labor movement.'

When I volunteered for the local of the hotel workers' union in San Francisco, something I've done on and off for the last two years, there was a contract fight going on, and my job was to get big hotel customers – academic conferences, corporate meetings – not to cross a picket line. Doing so meant first appealing to their sense of solidarity, and then, when that inevitably failed, suggesting that their conference could potentially be ruined by bullhorns and screaming picketers. I had frustrating phone calls with junior academics, who were usually paralyzed by inaction, who wanted to do the right thing that they'd read about in books, but at the crucial moment found themselves constitutionally unable to do the right thing in real life; it was hard for them to see the relationship between their adjunct, benefitless status and the healthcare issues facing a hotel worker. On the line outside a hotel, handing out leaflets, I struggled to impress upon a German visitor the fact that a worker's struggle here had relevance to his situation as a worker in Germany. Genosse, I started, taking his hand, but he walked promptly into the hotel.

The young radicals of Silicon Valley were the most disturbing: startup hackers skateboarding through picket lines, covered in piercings and tattoos, praying that tonight would be the night that they would get bought out by Microsoft, before investors would realize their company had no actual revenue and lay them off. They took our leaflets, crumpled them, and threw them back at us. A tourist from Indiana stopped me for a long conversation about how his furniture company was able to compete with China because it didn't have unions. It paid minimum wage and no benefits. As soon as I began to respond with what I knew about China – how badly workers were treated there, how violently the number of labor protests had skyrocketed this year – he shook my hand and walked into the hotel. I pondered the meaning of that hand-shake as I looked over to see a young man, who looked barely out of college, stopping at the line. He raised his fist and joined the chants; then he asked for some leaflets and started to hand them out. When we asked him why he had joined us, he said, ruefully, that he had just lost his job.

Benjamin Kunkel

– Political Psychopathology –

O ur unanimous opinion in favor of freedom of expression conceals a certain confusion between
two main rationales. The first is negative: because everyone has a right to speak, speech should go uncensored
and unpunished. The second principal rationale is a
positive one: unconstrained expression is not only freedom *from* official persecution but also freedom *to* consider all points of view. And, as with our adversarial
system of justice, the exchange of opposing arguments
is thought to beat a path to the truth. This second rationale figures much more prominently than the first in
the classic vindication of freedom of expression in John
Stuart Mill's *On Liberty*. Mill was of course a philosopher, and in essence he conceived of democracy as a
philosophical method: 'Complete liberty of contradict-
ing and disproving our opinion, is the very condition
which justifies us in assuming its truth for purposes of
action; and on no other terms can a being with human
faculties have any rational assurance of being right.'
Free expression, in other words, doesn't just protect
all speech but tends to improve its general truthfulness
and rationality. Touchingly, Mill seems to imagine a
society escaping from the dismal hush of censorship,

through a period of noisy argument, into a new quiet produced, this time, by rational accord: 'As mankind improve, the number of doctrines which are no longer disputed or doubted will be constantly on the increase: and the well-being of mankind may almost be measured by the number and gravity of the truths which have reached the point of being uncontested.'

Mill's essay today sounds both antique and contemporary. Pre-Freudian and pre-Edisonian, it doesn't consider the possibility of deep psychic attachments to error or, naturally, the manipulations of opinion enabled by photography, radio, film, TV, and, these days, electronic audiovisuals of all kinds. (An account of the special power of these media would begin with two observations: their production and distribution is more easily concentrated in a few hands than that of written language, and, being partly non-verbal, these media more easily circumvent rational consideration.) And yet Mill is also contemporary, or at least current: debates around the First Amendment continue to take place with allusions to his arguments and even invocations of his name.

In its 2009 *Citizens United* decision, the Supreme Court described free speech as 'the means to hold officials accountable to the people.' Moreover, the 5-4 majority added, quoting a prior opinion, political speech is 'indispensable to decision-making in a democracy, and this is no less true because the speech comes from a corporation.' This was an argument, then, not so much about the right of corporations, construed as people, to say what they like regardless of effects, but about the usefulness of corporate speech to the citizenry. The Supreme Court, composed of political appointees whose task is rationalization, not reasoning, may have been cynical in its arguments; but it paid homage to a venerable ideal in claiming that untrammeled corporate expression (which involves soundtracks and visual images as much as literal 'speech') would improve the intellectual judgment of citizens and the practical decision-making of their representatives.

Last year Jane Mayer wrote a story for the *New Yorker* about a wealthy North Carolina businessman named Art Pope, who, thanks to the *Citizens United* decision, bankrolls a few nominally independent political groups that run ads promoting Republican and attacking Democratic candidates for state office. Pope says about himself: 'Politically, I would describe myself as conservative, and philosophically I would describe myself as a classical liberal, which you had in John Locke, Adam Smith, and John Stuart Mill.' Yet the messages Pope emits into the public sphere, on the basis of his private wealth, aren't arguments in their best forms, as Mill imagined would come to prevail, but lies. One TV ad suggested that a Democrat who voted to cut spending on a Shakespeare festival was *increasing* the budget for such 'pork projects,' since he didn't try to eliminate arts funding altogether. Another ad portrayed a Democrat who supports the death penalty as eager to let murderers off death row. A veteran state senator named Margaret Dickson was also targeted by one of Pope's groups: 'They used an actress who has dark hair who was fair, like me. She was putting on mascara and red lipstick. She had a big ring and a bracelet.' The narrator of what Dickson called 'the hooker ad' then intoned 'Busted!' as the actress's hand grabbed a wad of bills. (Of course the US system of campaign finance requires that *all* politicians be hookers or rent boys, who sell their favors for cash; but a tidy combination of misogyny and hypocrisy means that the systemic scandal appears here only as a sexual smear against a particular woman.)

These TV spots may be unusually philistine, homicidal, and sexist. In other respects they are typical of contemporary American political speech as it appears in those fora to which citizens have most access, at least as spectators: debates, press conferences, speeches, political advertisements, cable TV, talk radio. Campaign strategists, pundits, politicians, and Super PACs tend to be as dishonest and vacuous as they can get away with, and at the level where the public sphere is most truly public we rarely if ever encounter an argument – say, that the US should invade Iraq, or balance the federal budget – in anything resembling its most articulate, rational, and best-documented form, let alone one set against the opposing case in *its* highest form. Arguments, to call them that, instead obey two main rules: misrepresent your own position, and misconstrue your opponent's. So the public sphere (again, where it's most open to the public as spectators, contemporary democracy being little more than a spectacle) represents policy in particular and the world in general not through rational discussion but by way of lies, fantasies, innuendo, and at best categorical propositions that no one bothers to defend and that are probably mere smoke screens for other propositions.

In math class they ask you to show your work, so that if you get the wrong answer you can later see where you went astray. In American political life today, you never show your work. So the answer to any question we take to be code for a hidden *dream-work*, to use Freud's term for the impacted logic of dreams. In this way, for instance, even Mitt Romney's pledge to relieve mass unemployment by cutting taxes for 'job-creators,' in the question-begging term, seems to refer not to any underlying economic theory, which he would never in any case elaborate, but to a concealed preference for the rich to get richer. Such a motive is not even, however, comprehensibly economic, since Romney himself is so rich already; it could only emerge out of some obscure compound of class-loyalty, self-admiration, cultural nostalgia, power hunger, or other elements altogether. Romney would anyway deny the motive we impute to him, and his denial might be sincere. The point is only that if we listen to his words – or to almost any contemporary political speech – we find ourselves not in the position of a rational interlocutor, but in that of a shrink faced with a patient: here is a someone who either doesn't believe what he says or says it for other reasons than he gives, and yet whose real reasons and motives are inaccessible to us, and may be to him, too.

Not that politicians and pundits are mentally ill in a clinical sense, but politics in American national life today can only be presented in pathological form. Politics no longer involves the public use of reason; it is instead a matter of psychopathology, and is already treated as such by politicians and the public alike. Only this can account for the political centrality of the 'gaffe' or slip of the tongue, an eminence that verbal inadvertencies have not enjoyed since the early days of psychoanalysis. But verbal or other symbolic blunders (Michael Dukakis looking not macho but dweeby in a battle tank; George W. Bush standing before a hubristic MISSION ACCOMPLISHED banner) are only the raw material or starting point for the practice of politico-psychopathology. The end result is an analysis – usually an accusation – of the 'true' meaning not only of a politician's words but of his hidden nature and undisclosed program. Almost invariably the true meaning reveals a taboo intention or identity.

Thus Obama, saying to business owners 'You didn't build that' to remind them of the government's role in providing infrastructure and educating the workforce, is in fact a Marxist who subscribes to the labor theory of value. Or Romney and Ryan, for all their libertarian talk of economic freedom, would, if elected – as Vice

President Biden said to an audience in Virginia – 'put y'all back in chains,' being adherents of the slavery theory of value. These slurs then become fodder for the same operation as performed by the other side. To brand the mildest talk of economic fairness as socialist, we liberals or leftists believe, surely shows radicalism not of the Democrats but of the Republicans. The Republicans for their part complain that allusions to the obscenity of slavery are the real obscenities which, in the words of the Romney campaign, 'disgrace the office of the Presidency' (already, in the subliminal implication, disgraced by a man who, by reason of his African descent, had no right to it in it the first place).

There exist both plausible and implausible, fair and unfair, interpretations of the occult significance of banal political speech. Either way, politics these days often consists of such interpretations, and is always potentially the *object* of such interpretations. The general procedure is virtually classical in its psychoanalytic logic. From the symptom (the telltale slip) we proceed to diagnosis (of the underlying sickness) and from the diagnosis to the remedy, which, since our opponents are always terminal cases – here we depart from standard clinical practice – can only be their banishment and defeat.

A tricky thing about this otherwise simple, not to say tedious game is that it's played at once by cynics and crazies, or people who are cynical one moment and crazy the next. Sometimes, in other words, my diagnosis of the other person is a deliberate and cynical misconstrual of his words (I know he doesn't actually believe *that*, but it's convenient to pretend he does) and sometimes it is a sincere exercise in politico-psychopathology (I *do* think he believes that, though he refuses to admit it, except by accident); and the same holds true for my opponent when he talks about me. But true craziness is fundamental, while cynicism is only tactical. This leaves the citizen-clinician with two tasks: to attempt to discern the distinct pathologies that animate American's two main political parties, and to guess at the sane (if contemptible) programs that must, at other times, motivate their common cynicism.

According to Adorno, in psychoanalysis only the exaggerations are true. If you wished to characterize the Democrats and the Republicans in terms of true exaggerations, you might say that the Republicans have become the Party of Psychosis while the Democrats have become the Party of Neurosis. The Republicans are psychotic because they have lost contact with reality, and orient their behavior not toward realities but toward fantasies. The Democrats are neurotic because they are aim-inhibited, as an old-fashioned shrink might say: their anxieties, hang-ups, and insecurities mean that they can't attain satisfaction, since in a basic way they won't even allow themselves to know what they want.

Many features of the Republican psychosis are well known: Global warming isn't caused by humans;

Fannie Mae and Freddie Mac are responsible for the financial crisis; the President, who may be a foreign-born anticolonialist undermining America at the bidding of his father's ghost, has eliminated the work requirement for welfare; and so on. There's never much point in talking to psychotics, though we can speculate about the particular delusions they exhibit. Most of us probably subscribe to an interpretation of the Grand Old Psychosis (GOP) that goes something like this: The trauma of American decline as experienced by white people, older people, and men – and above all older white men – has caused a psychic break producing a classic paranoid delusion, in which that segment of the population which through its race, culture, and creed embodies the American virtues responsible for the country's former greatness is being attacked by a composite monster (dark-skinned, sexually deviant, non-Christian, and anticapitalist) bent on stigmatizing family as patriarchy, religion as ignorance, and free enterprise as predation. Here as in many cases of persecution delusion we might suspect the displacement onto others of a terrible guilt, in this instance surrounding war, racism, climate destruction, and so on. This interpretation of Republican loss of contact with reality is cartoonish and speculative but, in my considered opinion as a democratic ecosocialist and citizen–clinician, probably true as far as it goes.

Yet many Republicans must only be psychotic north-by-northwest. This is our impression of a figure like Mitt Romney, who will say that he's unsure about anthropogenic climate change or make a joke about Obama's birth certificate but is assumed to know better. The genuine creed of the fake psychotics we suspect to be what one might call patriarchal militarist libertarianism: The role of government should be restricted to enforcement of contracts and the maintenance of public order, with exceptions made for the control of women's bodies and the bombing of foreign countries. Still, there's no reason to talk to Republicans about any of this. Faced with an outright lunatic or someone who insists on imitating one, you can only hope he goes back on his meds, jumps out a window, or (as the Republican base is doing today) dies of old age. An early principle of psychoanalysis was that psychosis couldn't be treated with the talking cure, while neurosis could be. The first proposition at least seems to have been correct.

Clinical psychiatry no longer uses the term *neurosis*, but it remains a vivid word. As Freud summarized the condition: 'The ego has come into conflict with the id in the service of the super-ego and of reality.' The neurotic has the feeling that he wants something, can't say what it is, and nevertheless is frustrated not to get it. Satisfaction having been foreclosed long ago, he becomes a kind of hesitant, recessive, bemused personality. You might think of Woody Allen but it would do just as well to picture Al Gore, John Kerry, or Barack

Obama. We liberal or left-wing citizen–clinicians feel that these men are decent, intelligent, and somewhat principled – that their desires are basically the right ones, their intentions more or less good – but that in the service of reality they must ignore the desires latent in their (and our) political unconscious. In deference to a punitive public superego, they sweep under the rug their real urges – which we'd like to think are for truth and justice – and thus come across, in classic neurotic fashion, as more or less castrated. In a way, the citizen–clinicians of the GOP agree with us: they too suspect that Obama is a radical at heart. The difference is that we doubt whether Obama is in communication with his heart anymore.

Unlike the Democratic neurotic, the Democratic cynic would *not* harbor unacknowledged political desires. He would instead be a mild upper middle-class reformist, basically content with society as it is, only feeling that it could attain its ideal form with a few more charter schools and/or somewhat fewer uninsured people. This is a person so morally and intellectually null, so libidinally feeble, with so little to repress, that his inner life is more difficult to imagine than a serial killer's. But let us suppress a shudder and suppose that such people exist throughout the center left.

The main tactic of both parties, in any case, and of all political camps, is the same: anathematization of the opponent on grounds of taboo-violation. Whether or not we sincerely believe that our opponents believe and practice vile crazy things, we must claim that they do. (For my part, I do think the Republicans believe and practice vile crazy things, while I consider the Neuro-tocrats mainly pathetic and confused, even when vile.) Here the realm of anthropology is superimposed onto that of psychoanalysis. At no point do we cross into the territory of liberal democracy as imagined by Mill or Habermas; we stray instead through a weird, uncanny zone where we can tell which side people are on not by the reasons they advance but by their *propagation and violation of taboos.*

Anthropologists explain that taboo-violators appear unclean, tainted; and someone who flouts a tribe's taboo ultimately can't belong to that tribe or never did. For this reason it will be implied, as in 2008, that Obama pals around with terrorists, or, as in 2011, that the Occupy movement is pervaded by anti-Semitism. Or that a candidate winks at murder or (like Romney the private-equity warlock) afflicts people with cancer, or is a prostitute of the sexual instead of legislative kind. If once upon a time people imagined a public sphere of more or less reasonable and honorable people leading one another toward ever greater reasonableness, this entailed a tacit anthropological specification: namely, that the citizens of a liberal democracy belong, as it were, to the same tribe or people. Not so today, when the object of politics is to place your opponent in another and non-American tribe entirely, defined by its repugnant customs and insane beliefs. To be associated, fairly or not, with terrorism or socialism or murder or slavery is to be polluted, and with the polluted there can be no real dealings. (This may explain the American fixation on adultery, conventional marriage being organized around just this taboo.)

Not that the half of the electorate that casts a ballot – and isn't thwarted by new laws suppressing the vote of minorities and the poor – necessarily believes the innuendos in ads and sound bites. But pollution-by-association may be effective anyway. If every time my name came up, my friends were shown a picture of some off-putting sexual or dietary practice, they wouldn't all want to hang out with me anymore. In the same way, depictions of the electoral Other's depravity – whether lies or only half-lies – reinforce at once the lunacy of the psychotics (who are confirmed in their mad beliefs), the caution of the neurotics (who are reminded of how quickly they would be shamed for revealing a genuine desire), and the cynicism of the cynics. For the cynical politician, his repetition of lying accusations may, helpfully, turn him into a genuine psychotic: as Hannah Arendt pointed out in 'Truth and Politics' (1967), '[T]he more successful a liar is, the more likely it is that he will fall prey to his own fabrications. . . Current moral prejudice tends to be rather harsh in respect to cold-blooded lying, whereas the often highly developed art of self-deception is regarded with great tolerance and permissiveness.' Not only will the apparently self-deceived politician be more readily forgiven than the plainly dishonest one, as with those who promoted the fabricated casus belli for the Iraq War, but he will retail his falsehoods more effectively. The cynical citizen – whose role is not to tell lies but to listen to them – will, on the other hand, merely feel his cynicism deepen. The subject of repeated attempts at brainwashing, as Arendt noted in the same essay, is more likely to stop believing anything than to go over to fanaticism.

None of us on the left can want to be psychotics estranged from reality or neurotics exiled from desire. And because we are contemporary American leftists it's impossible for us to be cynics in the sense of wanting power for its own sake: no one like that would enlist with such a marginal, ill-defined, and disorganized cause. What psychology can we develop, then, that would place us in line both with the reality principle and the pleasure principle?

The Republican psychosis hardly concerns us in any practical way. Arendt, to cite her once more, warned forty-five years ago that politics increasingly took place in 'a world without facts,' and the GOP bears out her prophecy every day. Fake news outlets respond by mocking the crazy fantasies, and journalists by fact-checking the cynical lies. But it's a mark of Gradgrind's philistinism in *Hard Times* when he says, 'Facts alone are wanted in life. Plant nothing else, and root out everything else.' Facts are *not* all that's wanted in a reality-based community; they only acquire meaning within a structure of narrative and desire. The elaboration of such a structure – analytic in retrospect, utopian in prospect – is, of course, just what the Democratic neurosis precludes. It is also what the left needs to do. After all, to know your mind it's not enough just to reject the craziness of others; you also have to ask what your own sanity would entail.

The relative ideological coherence of the right has given it an inestimable advantage in recent decades. The right's analysis of American decline was as clear as it was false: excessive government deserved the blame for its interference with the market and its unfair promotion of racial minorities and single women. The right's utopia, a lodestar for its policies, was also magnificently lucid, if often hypocritically advanced: liberation of the market would secure the best social outcomes, in terms not only of aggregate wealth but its concentration in deserving hands and its promotion of 'the traditional family,' reliant now on two adult incomes.

The left, with more honesty and intelligence, can tell its own story about American fortunes since 1968. And we also have, at least latently, a utopia to promote. Our retrospective analysis of course centers on neo-liberalism as a project of class domination (and, in the US, white and masculine domination) and the upward redistribution of wealth, in which all institutions of American society have been made to conspire: from banks and businesses to courts, schools, and jails. Our utopian project is much less well defined. It may be possible, though, to suggest a few lineaments. Ecology is more fundamental than economics or politics, since no society can accomplish what its natural environment and resource base won't allow – and, ecologically, our first principle would be long-term sustainability. After ecology, as a matter of logical though not necessarily political priority, comes economics, since the wealth and income of a society set limits on what society as a whole and its individual members can do. In the service both of overall prosperity and individual fulfillment, we want a far more equal distribution of wealth, with a minimum income for everyone, as well as, probably, a maximum for anyone; the total income of society would meanwhile derive from full employment. As for positive political freedoms, the rights to health care and education (through college) as free public goods would be insisted on. As for negative political liberties, we would demand the repeal of War-on-Terror offenses against civil freedoms, the end of mass incarceration, and the restored right to assemble (as denied by Bloomberg's New York and many other municipalities over recent years). Another item is the creation of public fora that make freedom of expression an actual capacity of citizens rather than a mere alibi for corporate dominion over speech. Our current difficulty in imagining how this last right – of genuine free expression – could be specified and enforced offers one explanation for why the rest of the program, easier to imagine, still seems like such a pipe dream. To whom could we address our minimalist sketch of utopia? Our small portion of the public can hardly communicate with the preponderant remainder, even to be jeered at.

This means that we can't begin debating the outlines of our utopia in the immediate hope of achieving 'truth for purposes of action.' At the moment our own political speech rests more squarely on negative justifications for free expression: it's part of a person or a movement's dignity to be able to know and say what it wants, with or without hope of satisfaction. Besides, as both psychoanalysis and ordinary conversation teach, speaking your mind often comes before knowing it. It would therefore be worth talking about the society we on the left want, no matter what we're likely to get. Nor can a movement without a program have much hope of implementing one, should history provide an opening, as it just might do.

We know, after all, that history consists largely of surprise turns and unexpected consequences. But this law is so easy to forget that illustrations of it – as well as of the chance usefulness of little magazines – are always welcome. The other day I came upon the following passage in William Morris's short essay 'How I Became a Socialist' (1894):

When I took that step, I was blankly ignorant of economics; I had never so much as opened Adam Smith, or heard of

Ricardo, or of Karl Marx. Oddly enough I *had* read some of Mill, to wit, those posthumous papers of his (published, was it in the *Westminster Review* or the *Fortnightly*?) in which he attacks Socialism in its Fourierist guise. In those papers he put the arguments, as far as they go, clearly and honestly, and the result, so far as I was concerned, was to convince me that Socialism was a necessary change, and that it was possible to bring it about in our own days.

– Contributors –

Elif Batuman is a senior writer at *n+1* and author of the essay collection *The Possessed*.

Carla Blumenkranz is a co-editor of *n+1*.

Kristin Dombek teaches in the Princeton Writing Program.

Keith Gessen is a founding editor of *n+1* and author of the novel *All the Sad Young Literary Men*.

Mark Greif is a founding editor of *n+1* and assistant professor of literary studies at The New School.

Elizabeth Gumport is a senior editor of *n+1* and graduate student in American Studies at Harvard.

Chad Harbach is a founding editor of *n+1* and author of the novel *The Art of Fielding*.

Benjamin Kunkel is a founding editor of *n+1* and author of the novel *Indecision*.

Marco Roth is a founding editor of *n+1* and author of the memoir *The Scientists*.

Nikil Saval is a co-editor of *n+1*.

Emily Witt is the author of a forthcoming book about the sex lives of American women.

Wesley Yang is the author of a forthcoming book from W. W. Norton.

nh Notting Hill Editions

Notting Hill Editions is devoted to the best in essay writing. Our authors, living and dead, cover a broad range of non-fiction, but all display the virtues of brevity, soul and wit.

Our books are only part of our offering. Our commitment to reinvigorating the essay as a literary form extends to our website, where our Essay Journal is regularly updated with newly commissioned short essays as well as news and opinions on essay writing. The website also hosts a wonderful Essay Library, a home for the world's most important and enjoyable essays, including the facility to search, save your favourites and add your comments and suggestions.

To discover more, please visit
www.nottinghilleditions.com